SAS

THE HISTORY OF THE SPECIAL RAIDING SQUADRON 'PADDY'S MEN'

About the Author

Stewart McClean served in 102 (Ulster) AD Regiment (V) as Battery Quartermaster BQMS. This unit was the successor to a number of Northern Ireland-based Gunner regiments, including 8th (Belfast) HAA Regiment into which Robert Blair Mayne was first commissioned in 1939. Mayne was appointed to 5 Light AA Battery which was raised in Newtownards, the author's home town. These facts have contributed to Stewart McClean's long-time interest in the wartime career of Blair Mayne, known as 'Paddy' to all who served with him. In 1997 a memorial was dedicated in Newtownards and the author was a member of the group that campaigned for this tribute to a local hero. As he explains in his introduction, this was also the occasion that sparked his interest in the Special Raiding Squadron, an SAS unit whose members were proud to call themselves 'Paddy's Men'. He currently lives in Northern Ireland.

SAS

THE HISTORY OF THE SPECIAL RAIDING SQUADRON 'PADDY'S MEN'

STEWART McCLEAN

The History Press

Front cover illustration: Statue of Lt Colonel Blair (Paddy) Mayne, SAS, standing in Conway Square, Newtownards. (Martin Conroy/Alamy Stock Photo)

First published 2006 by Spellmount
This paperback edition first published 2024

The History Press
97 St George's Place, Cheltenham,
Gloucestershire, GL50 3QB
www.thehistorypress.co.uk

British Library Cataloguing in Publication Data.
A catalogue record for this book is available from the British Library.

ISBN 978 1 80399 694 3

Typesetting and origination by The History Press
Printed and bound in Great Britain by TJ Books Limited, Padstow, Cornwall

MIX
Paper | Supporting
responsible forestry
FSC® C013056
FSC
www.fsc.org

Trees for LYfe

Contents

Dedication

A statue was unveiled and dedicated on 2 May 1997 to the memory of Lieutenant-Colonel Robert Blair Mayne DSO★★★ in the town square of his hometown, Newtownards. The Earl Jellicoe KBE DSO MC unveiled the bronze statue before handing over to the Very Reverend Fraser McLuskey MC MA BD who performed the dedication. These two men were accompanied to the ceremony by a contingent of former members of the Special Air Service Regiment. I had the great privilege and honour of meeting one of those men, Mr Terry Moore MM, the following morning and the first thing that struck me about him was his absolute modesty. During our conversation, he informed me that it was the wish of many of the men that The Special Raiding Squadron should be given its rightful place in history and so, over the next two years, Terry was responsible for providing me with the means of gathering much of the information contained in these chapters. He personally ensured that countless doors were opened for me, many of which I could only ever have dreamed about. Terry also introduced me to many of his friends and former comrades who had served so gallantly with him during those dangerous and difficult times. On another occasion he made it possible for me to attend an annual reunion held in Hastings where he introduced me to all assembled as the person who would tell the true story, a very hard cross to bear.

I would also like to say thanks to the men, and their wives, who gave freely of their time, patience and considerable knowledge: David Danger, Alex Muirhead, George Bass, Sid Payne, Bob Francis, Bob McDougall, Arthur Thomson, Duncan Ridler, Reg Seekings, Derrick Harrison, Nick Thurston, Jack Nixon and Douglas Monteith. It became a labour of love and Terry was always just on the other end of the telephone. 'Moore here, how can I help?' was his cheerful greeting. Sadly he is no longer with us but I agree totally with a statement made to me by the late Alex Muirhead during one of our many conversations: 'I firmly believe that he is up there watching you.'

God bless, Terry and thank you.

Stewart McClean
Newtownards
September 2005

Acknowledgements

While my name will be seen as the author of this book there are some people who really must be acknowledged for their support and assistance. These include Paul Rea, who first introduced me to the pleasures of a day's research and a good meal; Derek Harkness for his continued support (at times he was behind me, beside and in front of me as required); and Richard Doherty who allowed me the use of his literary expertise and his considerable military knowledge. Mrs Christina McDougall is a formidable lady and I am grateful for her friendship and advice.

A special word of appreciation goes to my wife Carole, who has, perhaps, had to contend with more than most and is wholly responsible for this book being finished.

And, finally, my two children, Alan and Holly.

Stewart McClean
Newtownards
Co. Down
September 2005

Special Air Service
SONG OF THE REGIMENT

There was a song we always used to hear,
Out in the desert, romantic, soft and clear
Over the ether, came the strain,
That soft refrain, each night again,
To you LILI MARLENE, to you LILI MARLENE.

Check you're in position; see your guns are right,
Wait until the convoy comes creeping through the night,
Now you can pull the trigger, son,
And blow the Hun to Kingdom come,
And LILI MARLENE'S boy friend will never see MARLENE.

Twenty thousand rounds of tracer and of ball,
Forty thousand round of the stuff that makes 'em fall,
Finish your strafing, drive away,
And live to fight another day,
But LILI MARLENE'S boy friend will never see MARLENE.

Creeping into Fuka, forty planes ahead,
Belching ammunition, and filling them with lead,
A 'flamer' for you, a grave for Fritz,
He's like his planes, all shot to bits,
And LILI MARLENE'S boy friend will never see MARLENE.

Afrika Korps has sunk into the dust,
Gone are the Stukas, its Panzers lie in rust,
No more we'll hear that haunting strain,
That soft refrain, each night again,
For LILI MARLENE'S boy friend will never see MARLENE.

Lyric written by Col. 'Paddy' Mayne' (Lieutenant Colonel Robert Blair Mayne).
Sung to the tune of LILI MARLENE.

List of Maps

Chapter I

Changing Times

The Special Raiding Squadron was formed in the weeks leading up to the end of the campaign in North Africa, which came to a close on 12 May 1943, and comprised men and officers drawn from 1st Special Air Service Regiment. The formation of this particular unit could have been regarded as a compromise since many senior officers at General Headquarters in Cairo felt that 1st SAS had outlived its usefulness as a fighting force and should be disbanded. The men would then either be sent back to their own regiments, or posted to the remaining Commando units or the Royal Marines where all their exceptional skills and qualities could be put to much better use. There was also a very considerable element within the GHQ staff that disliked the thought of this small irregular unit, over whom they had little or no control, fighting their own separate wars. They saw its members as undisciplined mavericks rather than the effective fighting force into which they had developed. Rules that did not relate to their type of warfare were simply bent or broken with new and more appropriate ones replacing them. Perhaps the real reason behind the GHQ attitude was a perceived threat to authority from some of the new ideas and methods that had begun to appear on, and off, the battlefields.

Nearing the end of 1942 the Prime Minister, Winston Churchill, who was known to be an avid supporter of the commando and special forces' ethic, had asked the commanding officer of the Special Air Service, Lieutenant-Colonel David Stirling, to provide him with his thoughts and ideas regarding the future development of tactics. It is highly possible that some people, on reading Stirling's communication, may have heard alarm bells starting to ring very loudly. The contents of the letter, which was classified as secret, envisaged the officers who commanded the SAS taking overall charge of all forthcoming special operations; the soldiers who formed the other units involved would then either be absorbed into their ranks or, at least, be controlled by them.

MOST SECRET.

PRIME MINISTER

1. I venture to submit the following proposals in connection with the re-organization of Special Service in the Middle East. ("Special Service" may be defined as any military action ranging between, but not including, the work of the single agent on the one hand, and on the other the full scale combined operation.)

(1) That the scope of "L" Detachment should be extended so as to cover the functions of all existing Special Service units in the Middle East, as well as any other Special Service tasks which may require carrying out.

(2) Arising out of this, that all other Special Service units be disbanded and selected personnel absorbed, as required, by "L" Detachment.

(3) Control to rest with the officer commanding "L" Detachment and not with any outside body superimposed for purposes of co-ordination, the need for which will not arise if effect be given to the present proposals.

(4) "L" Detachment to remain hitherto at the disposal of the D.M.O. for allocation to Eighth, Ninth and Tenth armies for specific tasks [Ninth Army served in Palestine and Tenth in Iraq]. The planning of operations to be carried out by "L" Detachment to remain as hitherto the prerogative of "L" Detachment.

2. I suggest that the proposed scheme would have the following advantages:

(1) Unified control would eliminate any danger of overlapping, of which there has already been more than one unfortunate instance.

(2) The allocation to "L" Detachment of all the roles undertaken by Special Service units would greatly increase the scope of the unit's training, and thereby augment its value to all ranks, who will inevitably greatly gain in versatility and resourcefulness.

(3) The planning of operations by those who are to carry them out obviates the delay and misunderstanding apt to be caused by intermediary stages and makes for speed of execution which in any operation of this kind is an incalculable asset. It also has obvious advantages from the point of view of security.

Signed
David Stirling
9.8.42

But fate meant that Stirling's far-reaching and innovative plans would never be implemented. In late-January 1943 he was betrayed by a group of Arabs and captured by Germans while endeavouring to meet up with First Army in Tunisia. The detractors of the new form of warfare may then have concluded that with Stirling in enemy hands, and no longer able to use his considerable influence, or his wide circle of friends and contacts in high places to pull strings, they had been handed an ideal opportunity to make some radical changes. Thankfully for all those who had fought so hard throughout the desert campaign this was not allowed to happen. Had it done so, it surely would have ranked alongside some of the biggest military blunders of the Second World War.

The small band of élite, highly trained, highly motivated and mobile soldiers who had originally formed the SAS had been responsible for destroying considerable numbers of aircraft, vehicles and equipment as well as causing damage to roads, railways and communications. They had also destroyed some of the Axis' much-needed petrol and oil supplies, although the greatest damage to such supplies had been caused by the Royal Navy and Royal Air Force, which, using Ultra decrypts, had been able to destroy tankers en route to North Africa from Italy and Greece. The SAS's wide-ranging and highly successful activities had caused frequent disruption in the rear areas of the Axis forces in Libya and ensured that troops assigned to guard duties on vital installations remained on their mettle. On one raid, Blair Mayne, Stirling's second-in-command, is believed to have destroyed more enemy aircraft on the ground than any single RAF fighter ace of the war; the figure of over 100 enemy aircraft destroyed by Mayne exceeds the highest-scoring RAF ace by some thirty machines. However, the story that Mayne ripped control panels out of German aircraft with his bare hands is highly unlikely, especially when one considers the quality of German workmanship. One former SAS soldier did recall that Mayne pulled the control panel out of a *Regia Aeronautica* Fiat CR42 biplane while the soldier was underneath the aircraft looking for the fuel tank.

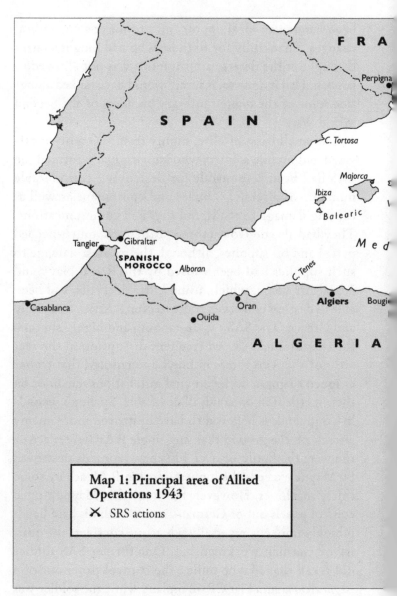

Map 1: Principal area of Allied Operations 1943
✕ SRS actions

Principal area of Allied Operations 1943

However, the exploits and heroic deeds of this small band of men were, and remain, the stuff of legend. Nothing, however outrageous it may have seemed to others, was beyond them as they roamed freely and fought the bewildered Axis forces at will. With their comrades of the Long Range Desert Group (LRDG) they became masters of hit-and-run tactics and, added to the destruction on the ground, and the tying up of German and Italian troops on guard duties, they also forced the Axis to deploy many men to scour the vast expanses of open and barren desert for their elusive attackers. Fear was also a major weapon in the SAS armoury; on many occasions even the thought of an attack on their positions caused widespread panic within the enemy ranks. News of the SAS success had reached the highest levels of the command structure in Nazi Berlin and, added to the many commando raids on mainland Europe, led Adolf Hitler to issue his infamous *Kommandobefehl* on 18 October 1942.

The Führer

SECRET

No. 003830/42g.Kdos.OWK/Wst   F.H. Qu

18.10.1942

12 copies

Copy No.12.

1. For a long time now our opponents have been employing in their conduct of the war, methods which

contravene the International Convention of Geneva. The members of the so-called Commandos behave in a particularly brutal and underhand manner; and it has been established that those units recruit criminals not only from their own country but even former convicts set free in enemy territories. From captured orders it emerges that they are instructed not only to tie up prisoners, but also to kill out-of-hand unarmed captives who they think might prove an encumbrance to them, or hinder them in successfully carrying out their aims. Orders have indeed been found in which the killing of prisoners has positively been demanded of them.

2. In this connection it has already been notified in an Appendix to Army Orders of 7.10.1942 that, in future, Germany will adopt the same methods against these Sabotage units of the British and their Allies; i.e. that, whenever they appear, they shall be ruthlessly destroyed by the German troops.

3. I order, therefore:-

From now on all men operating against German troops in so-called Commando raids in Europe or in Africa are to be annihilated to the last man. This is to be carried out whether they be soldiers in uniform, or saboteurs, with or without arms; and whether fighting or seeking to escape; and it is equally immaterial whether they come into action from Ships and Aircraft, or whether they land by parachute. Even if these individuals on discovery make obvious their intention of giving themselves up as prisoners, no pardon is on any account to be given.

On this matter a report is to be made on each case to Headquarters for the information of Higher Command.

4. Should individual members of these Commandos, such as agents, saboteurs etc., fall into the hands of the Armed Forces through any means – as, for example, through the Police in one of the Occupied Territories – they are to be instantly handed over to the S.D.

To hold them in military custody – for example in P.O.W. Camps, etc., – even if only as a temporary measure, is strictly forbidden.

5. This order does not apply to the treatment of those enemy soldiers who are taken prisoner or give themselves up in open battle, in the course of normal operations, large scale attacks; or in major assault landings or airborne operations. Neither does it apply to those who fall into our hands after a sea fight, nor to those enemy soldiers who, after air battle, seek to save their lives by parachute.

6. I will hold all Commanders and Officers responsible under Military Law for any omission to carry out this order, whether by failure in their duty to instruct their units accordingly, or if they themselves act contrary to it.

(Signed) A Hitler

As a direct result of that order many from the regiment, the commandos and other special forces would suffer inhumane treatment and torture in France at the hands of the SS and Gestapo before being brutally murdered.

It took a week of very hard bargaining and talking throughout a series of meetings in Cairo by Major Mayne, where he used his negotiating skills to great effect, to gain his objective. Over the years it has been wrongly, and sometimes wilfully, implied that he stuttered and stammered through those meetings or was incoherent when speaking in front of senior ranks. The real truth of the matter was that he was a very softly spoken man who, nevertheless, could present his case very eloquently. Yet should the need arise force could be used when he felt that it was required or that it best suited his purpose. Although he had gained a first class university education, although he had not completed his studies when war broke out, came from a good social background and was well travelled, he was neither a member of the upper class nor the landed gentry and in some quarters the old boys' network still prevailed. Or possibly it was due to the fact that he did not, and would not, conform to many of the outdated views on how war should be fought that he was never regarded as a particular favourite. Mayne was also trying to come to terms with the death of his father, William, on 10 January 1943 and with the refusal by his superiors to allow him compassionate leave to attend the funeral. Almost certainly that would have weighed very heavily on his mind because his family played a hugely important part in his life.

However, he eventually managed to convince GHQ of how wrong the decision to disband the regiment would be. He had achieved his primary goal of keeping his men together as a fighting force and had also been given command of the newly-formed Special Raiding Squadron. It has been documented that David Stirling had managed to make contact with GHQ from captivity and recommend

Mayne to succeed him as commander but there could never have been any other choice; Mayne's personal record of mayhem and destruction caused to German and Italian forces spoke volumes. Added to his large catalogue of feats was the fact that while still only a lieutenant (temporary captain) he had been awarded the Distinguished Service Order for his bravery and leadership during raids on the desert airfields of Sirte and Tamit. The citation reads:

> At Sirte on 12/13 December 1941 this officer was instrumental in leading and succeeded in destroying, with a small party of men, many aeroplanes, a bomb dump and a petrol dump. He led this raid in person and himself destroyed and killed many of the enemy. The task set was of the most hazardous nature, and it was due to this Officer's courage and leadership that success was achieved. I cannot speak too highly of this Officer's skill and devotion to duty.

For a junior rank to be awarded the DSO is regarded as second only to the Victoria Cross.

It can, therefore, be asserted that without the timely intervention of Major Blair Mayne the Special Air Service would have been disbanded. As a prime mover during their hard won battles, it was only fitting that Mayne should be the man to lead them into the future.

Chapter II

A New Role

And so, during the early months of 1943, the next chapter in the history of the regiment was about to begin. Although they still had great respect for Stirling's original ideas and his considerable achievements, especially in the formation of the regiment, many, if not all, the soldiers and officers felt that it was only when Mayne took command that the pace really picked up. He established himself quickly as an outstanding and inspirational leader while his men trusted his judgement without question and were dedicated totally to him, which is almost certainly why they referred to themselves as 'Paddy's Men'. The young soldiers who had been among the first to volunteer for L Detachment were all intelligent, skilled individuals who had been hand-picked after rigorous and highly dangerous selection procedures and training exercises. That they would follow him anywhere without fear or question speaks volumes about just how Mayne was regarded by them. His men were also very aware that, while he fully accepted and understood that some lives would inevitably be lost during subsequent fighting, he would never allow them to be sacrificed or used as cannon fodder.

Mayne was responsible for instilling many fine qualities in his men but he constantly stressed one point to make sure that they were always very aware of it: 'Every man has to be his own saviour and has to be totally self sufficient.' To many that might have seemed a small and very simple statement but it contained an enormous meaning and would become the ethos for every man in the regiment, then and now. He was always thinking about the wellbeing of his soldiers as was illustrated during a rest break while driving through the desert on a mission. Terry Moore was resting beside a jeep when Mayne suddenly asked him: 'Now tell me, Moore, we've all just been wiped out and you're the only survivor – how would you get back to where we've just come from?' Without stopping to think, Moore answered: 'Well, I'd just follow the wheel tracks in the sand.' 'But there are no tracks left because the wind would have blown them all away.' Mayne lowered his voice and looked straight at the young soldier: 'You've got to think all the time.'

But, like it or not, changes were inevitable and as with every compromise there was a price to be paid. That price was to be a reduction in overall strength to somewhere in the region of 300/350 men of all ranks as well as a change of role: under the new title of Special Raiding Squadron they would become assault troops. In the eyes of many they would be more akin to shock troops. Without doubt Paddy Mayne would control how his men fought and performed in their upcoming battles but he knew that he had lost the right to choose their future battlefields.

Prior to David Stirling's untimely capture and Mayne's eventful meetings in Cairo, A Squadron 1st SAS had been transferred for further training to the Middle East Ski School at The Cedars in Lebanon. That move had been made as a precaution due to the strategic threat posed by the German advance in the Caucasus. Had there been a German southward move from that region British forces, including Mayne's Squadron, would have had to fight in the mountainous regions of Turkey, Iraq or Persia. Training complete, however, the Squadron returned to its desert base in Kabrit where, with the rest of the regiment, the soldiers were to be told of their future. The newly promoted Major Mayne awaited them and, as always, he was a man of swift action. Eager to get started before any other changes might be implemented, he briefed them all immediately on the outcome of his short stay in Cairo. He also informed them that he would select the officers and senior non-commissioned ranks whom he wanted to accompany him; he would leave it to the discretion of those officers and NCOs to choose their own men. As the assembled ranks dispersed they knew that, at least for the foreseeable future, those chosen would remain together. The following figure shows the command structure.

Squadron HQ Officers

Squadron Commander	Major R B Mayne DSO
Second-in-Command	Major R V Lea (struck off strength, Palestine, 8 Aug '43)
Admin Officer	Captain E L W Francis
Medical Officer	Captain P M Gunn
Intelligence Officer	Captain R M B Melot

Padre	Captain R G Lunt (detached to SS Bde, 31 July '43)
Signals Officer	Lieutenant J H Harding (RFHQ, Palestine, 20 July '43)
Mortar Detachment Commander	Lieutenant A D Muirhead (A/Captain from 16 May '43)

No.1 Troop Officers

Troop Commander	Major W Fraser
Section Commander	Lieutenant J Wiseman (A/Capt from 6 Oct '43)
Section Commander	Lieutenant A M Wilson (A/Capt from 16 May '43)
Section Commander	Lieutenant C G G Riley

No.2 Troop Officers

Troop Commander	Captain H Poat (A/Major and Sqn 2 i/c from 8 Aug '43)
Section Commander	Captain T Marsh
Section Commander	Lieutenant P T Davies
Section Commander	Lieutenant D I Harrison (A/Captain from 8 Aug '43)

No.3 Troop Officers

Troop Commander	Captain D G Barnby (Apptd Adjutant 8 Aug '43)
Section Commander	Captain E Lepine (Apptd Tp Comd vice Barnby 8 Aug '43)
Section Commander	Lieutenant M H Gurmin (Struck off strength, Palestine, 8 Aug '43)
Section Commander	Lieutenant J E Tonkin

Their new role meant that there would be a large influx of new soldiers who would have to be integrated quickly into the various sections and apprised of the regiment's methods. These men would be drawn from all parts of the Army and their skills as signallers, drivers, engineers and medics were much needed. But not all the new arrivals would be totally unfamiliar. Sid Payne was a member of the Special Boat Squadron but felt that he was due for a change.

I simply packed my kitbag and waited in Cairo for Paddy and his squadron to return. I approached him and simply asked if it would be alright for me to join his men. He told me that he could think of no reason why not and said that it should be fine. He also told me not to worry as he would see to all the necessary paper-work. So I just jumped onto the back of a lorry and that was that.

But, despite all the upheavals, things moved along at a considerable pace and within a week a small advance party under the command of one of the recently arrived officers, Lieutenant Derrick Harrison, had been despatched to set up a new camp and make things ready for the arrival of the rest of the troops.

The main body of the newly established Squadron travelled up from Egypt by train and, almost immediately after their arrival, began a period of heavy and intensive training at their new base at Az Zib, a small, remote village in northern Palestine close to the Syrian border. Although there were some small buildings that could be used for storing essentials, the accommodation for the majority of the troops would be tents. It proved to be an almost ideal location since the hilly terrain and rocky areas surrounding the base provided excellent training areas. The soldiers laboured for many long hours learning how to handle and use the large scaling ladders, ropes and equipment needed for climbing cliff faces but, knowing only too well from experience that those items would not always be available to them, they went even further and practised climbing the rock faces using only their bare hands. As if the rigours of climbing were not difficult and arduous enough the decision was taken that this had also to be accomplished while carrying the full weight of personal equipment and weapons. When they felt that the conditions they were working under made it necessary, they also refined and rewrote the training manuals. On other occasions they devised new methods that they felt suited better their own personal needs; exceptional men required exceptional training. Nothing was left to chance and so all those highly demanding and dangerous exercises had to be carried out during both daylight hours and darkness. The construction and laying of explosive charges would be a new skill for some as would be the use of the many different types of fuses or time pencils needed for demolition work. The explosives training was placed under the control of a small section of Royal Engineers who had been attached to the Squadron.

However, a number of men who had seen action in the desert would have been old hands with improvised explosive devices as they had trained and fought alongside Jock Lewes who had invented a completely new type of sticky bomb for the destruction of enemy aircraft. As well as having the incendiary properties required for the job, its lightweight construction meant that more could be carried on raids. Lewes's invention became legendary and was rightly named after him, the Lewes Bomb. Another major priority for all concerned was learning how to handle and operate the various types of German and Italian weapons that they might encounter. Weapons were, after all, the tools of their chosen trade and quite a few preferred to use the German MP38/MP40 machine pistols when the chance arose. That particular weapon had an extremely good rate of fire and as the ammunition fired by it was substantially lighter they could carry larger quantities. While the Mk 4 Lee–Enfield was a thoroughly good rifle, and the mainstay of the British Army, its bolt action could be slow, even in the best of hands. It was also fairly heavy and cumbersome which was a disadvantage for close-quarter fighting. The Thompson submachine gun, more commonly known as the Tommy gun, was another preferred weapon and with either the 30-round box or 100-round drum magazine was good for tight situations, such as house clearance, where automatic fire often made the difference between life and death.

The Squadron's men knew that they would be travelling mainly on foot and so would be without their ubiquitous Willys jeeps. Those tough little vehicles had allowed them to carry their heavier weapons into many battles but their mainstay in the future for them would have to be the .303 calibre Bren gun. During their desert raids they would have carried somewhere in the region of a thousand rounds and twenty to thirty magazines with them aboard their jeeps. Those figures would have been greatly supplemented by what they had stashed away in various hiding places. But for physical and practical reasons they would have to make do with greatly reduced numbers of approximately 300 rounds and ten magazines per weapon. Each individual magazine had a capacity of only thirty rounds, although it was normal practice to load only twenty-eight rounds, but the gunners could put this firepower to devastating use. (The practice of loading the magazine with twenty-eight rounds was intended to extend the life of the springs that held the bullets firm in the magazine. When circumstances demanded, the full load could be used.) Each magazine was usually loaded with a mixture of the three types of rounds available: ball, tracer or armour piercing.

Compared to some of the machine guns used by the enemy the Bren had a relatively slow rate of fire at 500 rounds per minute but that was far outweighed by its superb accuracy and outstanding reliability. However, Paddy Mayne, who was regarded by all as an excellent shot, was forever berating and shouting at the gunners for firing in long bursts. He much preferred them to use controlled bursts or what was commonly known as double tapping, two shots in quick succession. Private Jack Nixon, a veteran of No.7 Commando before he joined the SAS, was one of those unlucky men who came under constant verbal attack for keeping his finger on the trigger longer than necessary. Because of the barracking he had to suffer, Jack was often heard muttering under his breath as he jokingly referred to Mayne: 'That man is the bane of my life.' Nixon's skill with the Bren was well known and his prowess would be heavily tested throughout the coming months. Private Douglas Monteith, another former commando who had served with No.8, was glad to note on many occasions that 'Jack was incredible with that thing and I was just glad that he was on our side and not shooting at us'.

Countless hours were spent training and carrying out practice drills until it all became second nature. Every aspect of daily routine, however trivial it might have appeared, was carried out at the express orders and under the watchful eye of Paddy Mayne who, to an outsider, might have appeared to be a ruthless tyrant who was utterly relentless as he constantly drove his men onwards. On many occasions they would be pushed extremely close to their personal limits but, as was common practice with him, Mayne took part in whatever happened and was the main driving force behind everything. At times it must have appeared to many of the new men that they were being treated like a bunch of raw recruits all over again. Even the most basic of subjects and skills had to be covered from scratch. Shooting and fieldcraft carried a great importance but it was absolutely vital that everyone knew how to map read using the stars and find a compass bearing. But, to their credit, the men never faltered or complained in the slightest because they understood only too well why all of that familiarisation and retraining was necessary.

The main core of the Squadron, its backbone, was made up of the battle hardened veterans who had survived the rigours of war in the desert. They had been taught, and absorbed, some very serious lessons over the last few years. Necessity had shown them the need for looking after and maintaining all their fighting kit as well as caring for themselves. Basic personal hygiene had always played a very large part in their daily lives and whenever possible they cleaned and washed their clothes. The severe deprivations encountered had also taught them the need to respect the psychological demands on their minds as well as the physical demands placed on their bodies. All those hard learned lessons stayed with them and proved on more than one occasion to be deciding factors in their successes and survival. One very important point that must also be taken into account is that, despite all the experience they had amassed, many of these men were still very young. The majority were still in their late teens or early twenties. Some like Jack Nixon and Titch Davison had actually lied about their ages when they had joined the Army; Nixon had only reached the tender age of 15 when he signed up.

Quite a few of the new soldiers who had recently joined the ranks had also to be put through their basic parachute training in order to gain their wings before being allowed to join a section. The jump training was no longer under their own control as it was being conducted by instructors from an airborne battalion based in Egypt. Tragically, one of the new men lost his life while making a practice descent. That incident would have caused Paddy Mayne to think long and hard as he would have remembered losing another two young men under similar circumstances. Wharburton and Duffy had been the first fatalities suffered by the fledgling L Detachment at Kabrit on 17 October 1941. Perhaps he recalled standing at the bar in The French Club at Ismailia shortly after their deaths and being asked if he thought that the two men might have lost consciousness before hitting the ground. He never even paused for thought as he gave his answer to that question: 'No, as I had to listen to their screams until they hit the ground.' It was a very quiet and sombre reply and no further comments were added.

Among the many arrivals at the training camp was a new padre, Captain Robert Lunt, and to the men that meant only one thing: Sunday morning religious services. On one Sunday morning parade Sergeant-Major Rose formed the squadron up into ranks and called them to attention: 'One step forward march all Jews and Muslims.'

He bawled out the order in his best parade ground voice. It was in no way meant to be derogatory; the simple fact was that their different faiths did not allow them to worship together. Rose was an old hand and obviously knew the score among the men only too well. So it came as no surprise in the least when to a man they all took the one pace forward. He also failed to take any notice of their widely grinning faces but stood his ground and remained poker-faced as he barked out further orders before marching them all off to the service.

The physical fitness side of their army life consisted of having to take part in the obligatory forced marches. That highly demanding and, at times, extremely dangerous form of training had to be carried out both during the day under a blazing sun and at night in freezing cold. It was gruelling exercise that took place alongside the usual training and drill although it must be said that drill and parade ground activities did not enjoy very high priority among the men of the Squadron. Sergeant-Major Doug 'Gus' Glaze was the physical training instructor (PTI) in charge of that side of things. His ways and methods were well known to many since he had also been responsible for training the original members of L Detachment at Kabrit. Sid Payne was among those who had already sampled his training and his description may have seemed strange to many outsiders.

It was not only interesting but also totally enjoyable, the type of training you received from Gus was definitely an experience. One minute you would be struggling to do some press ups and the next you would be lying on your back gasping for air through laughing too much. He was a very funny man who was never short of a story to tell.

Everyone, including officers, had to take part in his torturous training regimes and his only concession to officers was to include the word 'SIR' at the end of his scathing but friendly abuse. The soldiers who had undergone the desert training understood fully and appreciated the reasoning behind it. That meant that a comment like the one Sid had made was never regarded as out of place, even if they could not bring themselves to agree with the thinking behind it. The values and advantages of hard work and commitment earned more respect in the ranks than just being regarded as some sort of hard man in the brawling sense.

But, as time wore on, Sergeant-Major Glaze found it increasingly difficult to watch all his friends, whom he had made fighting fit, leave while he was left behind kicking his heels at base waiting to take charge of his next training session. Perhaps it was the friendly abuse directed at him or just his being subjected to name calling that finally made up his mind. After much thought he decided to give up his PTI's post to become an operational soldier. However, he was to find out, much to his discomfort, that there would be a price for making that choice. Despite the fact that he was an extremely well liked member of the Squadron, and a highly respected senior NCO, he had presented the men with an opportunity that was just too good to be missed. They decided to get their own back on him for all the physical and mental torture that he had put them through. So, because of his outstanding fitness and strength, the other soldiers loaded him up like a pack mule and gave him extra equipment to carry. While some men might have to carry three mortar rounds on top of their kit he would be given ten. But his punishment would not end there. Sicily was criss-crossed by hundreds of dry-stone walls that were about five feet in height. As he tried to climb over one of these he missed his footing and stumbled forward before falling, like a large bag of potatoes, flat on his face. Revenge was complete and obviously tasted sweet as Doug Glaze found himself the subject of a large amount of good-humoured abuse and laughter. The downside of that incident was that Glaze broke his ankle and missed the main action.

Before the outbreak of war Paddy Mayne had been very well known, and respected, as an outstanding rugby union player. He had played many games for his native province of Ulster, earned six caps for Ireland and toured South Africa with the British Lions in a highly successful campaign in 1938. During a period of leave from the Army he had spent some time in Liverpool watching a group of men training for rugby league and had been so impressed by their total commitment to the game, and their outstanding fitness, that he introduced it into his own training regime. The young soldiers who made up the Squadron already possessed a vast array of outstanding qualities. Those new skills that they had learnt, added to the levels of fitness that they achieved, combined to mean that they were second to none and ready to face anyone or anything.

However there was one particular quality displayed by many of his men that did not please their Commanding Officer at all: their grasp and abuse of the English language. It was widely known that Blair Mayne had an aversion to the use of foul or bad language. He was not a fool and knew and understood only too well that most men would, and did, swear at some stage when under pressure. That much he could manage to accept and overlook, but what he was totally against was that type of language being used in everyday conversations. While taking part in one of their many training sessions he suddenly stopped what they had been doing and called his men together before lashing in to them with his own long string of expletives: 'You see, I know just as many as you do, if not more, and even some you may possibly never have heard of before.' That was a very rare occurrence for him as he was not prone to making such a speech in public, except perhaps when he had indulged in a drink or two, and even then he was more likely to burst into song. His severe dressing down might not have stopped his men swearing but it certainly would have had the desired effect of reminding them to watch their Ps and Qs, at least when he was within hearing range.

On 13 May the Squadron learned that they would shortly be put to the test when Lieutenant-General Miles Dempsey, commander of XIII Corps, paid them a visit. Even though they had only been together for a relatively short time the men had been trained to perfection and were ready for anything. They were also extremely keen to hear any sort of news regarding action. They had been assembled very hurriedly and marched to the camp cinema to hear Dempsey's speech. However, it soon became obvious to the watching audience that he had not been very well informed about whom he was meeting and addressing. But Major Mayne spotted his blunder straight away and came to the rescue. He soon put the General on the right track with a few well-chosen words in his ear. After overcoming the initial embarrassment of talking to the men as if they were raw recruits Dempsey made his apologies. The next part of his address was what everyone in the crowded room had been hoping to hear. He informed them that they were soon to play a part in the forthcoming attack on southern Europe.

'I know that I need not impress on you the importance of succeeding in this task but I am confident you will succeed.'

Dempsey not only spoke to the men but took the time to join in with them and run the gauntlet of the live ammunition that was being fired during their training exercises. He witnessed some outstanding fighting and leadership qualities being displayed during his brief visit and the Squadron made a strong and lasting impression on him. His judgement was spot on and he would be proved to have been absolutely correct in that initial assessment by events throughout the forthcoming actions. An extremely astute and shrewd man, Dempsey was possibly one of the very few senior officers at that time who really knew and appreciated fully the extremely high calibre of the fighting men he had just encountered.

As he had watched the men going through their paces one young man in particular had caught his eye and he asked if he could possibly speak to him personally. Private Davison was called forward and asked to tell the General his age. 'Twenty-one, sir,' was his very curt and formal reply. Dempsey looked at the youth standing in front of him and found his answer hard to believe and so he asked the question again. His request was not for any military reasons; he was just interested and simply wanted to know. No different answer was forthcoming; he was met with the same short reply. However, on asking a third time he was told in not so many words that if he did not believe what he had just been told then he knew what he could do and also where he could go. In fact he had been fully justified in making the enquiry: the young soldier in question was only 17 years old and had lied about his age when he had joined the Army.

Titch Davison was a member of Sergeant Reg Seekings'
section and had earlier asked to be allowed to use one of
the section's Brens. Seekings turned down his request and
told him: 'Sorry son but a Bren gun is for killing, and I just
don't think that you could handle that particular job at this
point in time.' Although Davison understood the thinking
behind that remark he disagreed with it and told Seekings
that he felt he would be able to do it. Slowly he produced a
crumpled letter from his pocket and handed it over to Reg.
The letter was to inform him that his brother had just been
reported as having been killed in action. This was on top
of the brothers that he had already lost. He was immediately given the weapon and used it to great effect. Sadly he
would join his brothers when he became one of seventeen
men who lost their lives when their truck was blown up by
an enemy shell at Termoli.

Chapter III

Final Preparations

Levels of activity increased and there next followed an even more rigorous period of training and preparation. Included was the study of military tactics plus the planning and organisational skills needed to carry out the varying methods of attack. A new type of weapon was also added to the arsenal when 3-inch mortars were introduced to the Squadron. Once properly established and integrated these would provide the squadron with its own form of mobile artillery. The mortars would then be able to follow on either alongside or close behind the fast moving sections or even the individual troops. A mortar platoon of twenty-eight men was formed and put under the command of Lieutenant Alex Muirhead in Headquarter Squadron. Many of the soldiers who would man the mortars were drawn from those who had recently arrived and had little or no experience in the new tasks that would be required of them. Three-man teams were assembled and put through a thorough training and familiarisation regime with the new weapons. Once everything had been completed and the men had reached the high level of skill required they were able to sustain a high rate of fire; they could have thirteen rounds in the air before the first had even hit the ground and exploded. Rightly or wrongly, the men had been informed that the Germans had achieved that particular rate of fire and so they believed that if the enemy could do it then so could they. The one person who was perhaps happier than most with the excellent progress being made by his charges was their newly installed commander, Alex Muirhead. 'Obviously I had seen them before and knew what they were and what they could do, but I had absolutely no experience of using them.' Until he had been placed in charge of the platoon he had never even operated the weapon. But, needless to say, Muirhead realised that he had been given a specific job to do and there was no way that he was going to be found wanting. He was a highly intelligent young man and a fast learner who soon mastered the skills needed to control his men and direct the fall of their fire.

Everyone knew that their training was about to take another turn when orders were issued to pack their belongings and prepare for a move from their base in Palestine to the docks at Suez. The squadron and all its equipment made the long journey by road and as they arrived in the harbour area they got their first glimpse of the ever-growing armada. Very soon they would be ferried out to their latest billet, the *Ulster Monarch*. The choice of that particular vessel must surely have caused Mayne to smile as before the war it had plied its trade as a ferry between the ports of Belfast, in Northern Ireland, and Liverpool.

Much time and effort was to be put into learning the new skills required to make beach landings from landing craft assault (LCAs). They were assigned a flotilla of eight of those small craft, each of which when properly loaded was capable of carrying thirty-five fully equipped men and its own crew. A firm bond of friendship quickly developed between the sailors and the men of the Squadron over the next few months as they trained together. The huge figure of Paddy Mayne made a suitable impression on the seamen and, although maybe not to his face, some of them even referred to him as 'the mad Major Mayne, a giant Irishman and gentleman'. Due to the sense of mutual respect and friendship between them they were granted special permission by Mayne to carry the regiment's proud emblem, the Flaming Sword and the motto 'Who Dares Wins' on their small craft. A ship's carpenter was found who quickly made the required templates. After they were painted they became the only boats of their size in the Royal Navy to carry that famous insignia. In fact the sailors regarded it as such an honour that the emblems stayed emblazoned on their bows right through to the end of the war.

Training was hard and extremely strenuous but, as usual, everyone took it all in their stride to become accomplished in the art of beach landings. Once on board, they formed themselves into three lines with the men of the middle line having the unenviable task of spearheading the way onto the beach as soon as the armoured ramp was lowered. They worked long and hard to fine-tune all the necessary elements of the training by staging numerous mock attacks and landings along the Sinai coastline. The landing craft were flat bottomed and that caused them to be fairly unstable in all but the calmest sea conditions. Not everyone was lucky enough to be blessed with a strong stomach, which meant that quite a few men changed to a subtle shade of green on more than one occasion. Conditions on board were also basic and cramped and afforded very little cover or overhead protection for the occupants. Everyone was aware that they would be open to all that the elements and the enemy could throw at them. At one stage in training they even found themselves being towed along behind some of the larger ships. The objective of that strange exercise was to acclimatise them to any rough sea conditions that they might have to encounter.

The strict training and discipline regime to which they were subjected was very thorough and no one was spared. This was borne out in the following story told by Lance-Corporal Terry Moore, a member of C Section under Captain Tony Marsh. The three troops, A, B and C along with Headquarter Troop, had to take part in a forced march. Before setting out they had also been informed that any soldier who failed to complete the march would be sent back to his parent unit. The three dreaded and ominous words 'returned to unit' (RTU) carried with them a greater threat than any form of punishment or charge sheet ever could for those men. Needless to say, it would be extremely difficult as the route chosen meant that they would have to cover a distance of some forty-eight miles. It had also been designed to be carried out under the most severe climatic conditions. Each man was expected to carry his full complement of equipment, which could weigh in the region of sixty to seventy pounds. It was also common practice to ration strictly the allocation of drinking water. The quantity of water each man was allowed to have in his water bottle had been calculated carefully during the early days of L Detachment at Kabrit. Throughout the hours of daylight, temperatures in the desert were extreme and could be as high as 104–108° Fahrenheit while at night it could be well below freezing point.

Only about fifty per cent of the men from A Section and about seventy-eight per cent from B Section managed to finish the punishing march. All the members of C Section finished, although Bob Lilley had the almost back-breaking job of carrying one of his exhausted men draped across his shoulders for the last ten miles. Despite the immense hardships suffered by all concerned they still managed to double in for the last two miles. Spirits were very high as they halted, did a right turn and came smartly to attention. It was always that extra edge of competitiveness and rivalry that spurred that type of man to give just a little more than was required from him. The poor man who had suffered the misfortune of being carried back was never allowed to forget his unfortunate collapse as later on during their time aboard the *Ulster Monarch* a popular request to be played over the ship's loudspeaker system was a song entitled 'I'll walk beside you'.

Paddy Mayne made a point of completing the march with all his extremely exhausted troops. Bob McDougall watched him in utter amazement: 'One moment he could appear at the front of one Troop, then the middle of another. Next you could lose sight of him in the distance only to see him reappear leading the whole march.' But such an act of endurance did not surprise any of his men in the slightest as they had all come to expect it from him. That sort of happening was no act of bravado but routine practice for him, as he always led by example and the simple words 'It's OK lads, just follow me' were often heard. Derrick Harrison was only one of many to remark about his physical prowess and stamina:

'For such a large man he could cover the ground at an incredible speed.'

The terrible conditions and deprivations that they encountered could be totally mind numbing and, on occasions, very hazardous. As they slogged and sometimes dragged themselves along, the fine sand penetrated everything: boots, clothes and every orifice that it could possibly find. It also sapped the strength from their already tired legs and weary bodies, while the weight of their equipment forced them to sink knee-deep into the dunes. The heat from the blazing sun burnt right through their clothes and onto their skin. At times the dazzling glare made it nearly impossible for anyone to see which way they were meant to be going. Added to these hardships was the constant danger of sunstroke, temporary blindness or even permanent eye damage.

As if the sand and sun were not causing enough problems their tortuous route found them having to wade through countless rocky streams where one false move on the slippery rocks could mean broken bones. On many occasions the water they had to wade through would be flowing very fast and up to chest height. They were forced to navigate blindly through cornfields and large areas of rough and prickly scrub. Sharp thorns tore through any exposed flesh and often covered their heads, making it impossible to see anything. Vast outcrops of razor-sharp rocks that could easily rip through clothing, boots or bare skin stood in their way and had either to be climbed over or marched around. The men had pushed their bodies right to, and in some cases beyond, the limits of endurance and must have suffered incredible discomfort and pain.

But, more importantly, they had achieved what they had set out to do and despite the obvious aches and pains their immense pride and total belief in themselves had enabled them to overcome all the obstacles and succeed. A shattered, but very relieved, Bob McDougall was making his weary way down towards the waiting boats which would ferry them back out to *Ulster Monarch*. As he passed Major Harry Poat he stopped to take a quick look at the latter's feet as he was carefully removing his tattered boots. The sight that McDougall witnessed almost turned his stomach: 'It was more like looking at some overripe tomatoes than anything that resembled a pair of feet.' It later turned out that Major Poat had volunteered to try out a new type of canvas boot. While Sid Payne's feet had survived the rigours of the desert march, his hob-nailed boots had not. 'I decided to wear that pair instead of my normal rubbersoled boots, but when I took them off the sole came away in my hand. What made me feel even worse was that I had just paid good money to get them out of the menders.'

At the completion of the forced march the officer responsible for carrying out the recce was immediately taken aside and informed that he was being sent back to his unit. Instead of checking out the ground on foot, as he should have done, he thought that it would be smart and easier to employ an entirely different method. He carried it out on horseback. Rank could never be used as a cover or excuse with that type of man. They still adhered to the same rules that had been applied from the earliest days of their existence; all ranks were treated as equals, even when applied to something as simple as queuing for meals. However, there was never any particular malice shown or intended towards any men who had made mistakes or failed, nor were their shortcomings, of whatever nature, ever discussed openly. They simply had not measured up to the exacting standards of behaviour and conduct required, but at least they had shown the correct spirit in trying to become members of the Special Air Service Regiment. Perhaps Mayne's real feelings about rank were to be found in a comment made in a letter to his mother in late 1942: 'Incidentally I am a Major now, I must develop a red nose and a pompous manner'.

Two men who knew Paddy Mayne very well were Private Bob 'Mac' McDougall and Corporal Arthur 'Tommo' Thomson. Both recalled how, with just one piercing look, he was able to look at a man and immediately size up his character: 'It was just as if he was looking right through him.' That same fearful look could be used to wither a man on the spot. They knew only too well that on other occasions it could be seen as the warning sign for one of his famous black moods:

> Paddy was an incredible man in many ways but at times he could be extremely frightening to those who went up against him. He could also be very difficult to handle and like many of us he would sometimes go off on a large bender. Despite that his behaviour was no better or no worse than those of us who accompanied him.

Many others also remembered his aversion to fools or foolish behaviour. That trait could be used on officers, of whatever rank, as well as ordinary soldiers, or even civilians.

Mayne demanded high standards and was never afraid to tell the person in question just how he felt about them. During initial training at their desert base at Kabrit the then young Lieutenant Mayne had been placed in charge of the fledgling unit's discipline. But, as with most things in the regiment, this did not conform to the ordinary military practice of being placed on a charge. Even the long established act of standing in front of a commanding or senior officer differed greatly from normal practice. Many soldiers would have heard the familiar words 'Will you accept my punishment', but these took on a very different meaning when Mayne uttered them. If he answered 'Yes' the offending soldier was instructed to put on a pair of boxing gloves and take his punishment in the boxing ring.

Before the war Mayne had been a fighter of some renown and had won the Irish Universities' heavyweight championship. Needless to say, the justice meted out was of a very swift and extremely painful nature. He had huge hands and although predominantly right-handed his left hook was every bit as deadly. The powers that be would almost certainly not have approved of his methods but the men on the receiving end accepted it totally. Once the punishment had been carried out the details of their transgressions were quickly forgotten and never mentioned again. Many of the men around Mayne used the same methods to solve their own arguments or differences. They were extremely hard and tough individuals, although they could never be described as being brawlers, and each knew only too well that his life could often depend on the person fighting alongside him. Living and working so closely together meant that there could never be any room for friction. During conversations they quite openly and proudly referred to each other as 'hard hitters'. Friendships forged in many difficult situations remained intact but woe betide anyone else who overstepped the mark.

Although on occasions Mayne could be a strict disciplinarian who stuck rigidly to the letter of the law, he also displayed a tremendous sense of humour and loved nothing more than hearing someone spin a good yarn or tell a tall tale. On one occasion he had to deal with one of his men who had returned late to camp after being on leave. The offending soldier was marched in and brought to attention in front of him.

> Well sir you see it was like this, I had honestly left in plenty of time and was making my way back so I decided that it would be all right to stop for a quick fag. The wind was blowing fierce hard in my face so I just turned around to light it. But then I forgot about that and just started to walk again. Before I knew what had happened I was back where I had come from.

That highly colourful and original explanation obviously did the trick as it was accepted. Mayne, however, was no one's fool and would have been in little doubt that he had just been told a rather large cock-and-bull story; but even he had to admit that it was, after all, an interesting and highly entertaining excuse.

Even during training exercises the pace of the daily routine on board their floating home never slackened as they were subjected to constant weapon and kit inspections. Boat drills were regularly carried out alongside the difficult task of learning how best to use the cumbersome cargo nets and rope ladders.

Nearing the end of their training General Bernard Montgomery boarded *Ulster Monarch* to pay the Special

Raiding Squadron a visit and give them a pep talk. He spoke briefly to his assembled audience and forcibly urged them on more than one occasion to 'kill Germans, kill Germans'. As he reached the end of his speech he wished them all the best of luck before turning to take his leave. As the entourage started to make its exit a rousing cry of 'Three cheers for Monty' went up from one of his aides. This was greeted with a deafening and rather embarrassing silence. Perhaps no one had heard the request so yet another such call was made. It brought exactly the same result. One young soldier by the name of Douglas Monteith decided that he had been given an opportunity that was just too good to be missed. He immediately jumped up onto one of the ship's capstans and turned to face his somewhat bemused comrades, pausing briefly for maximum effect before taking a very theatrical bow. When asked what he thought that he was doing, his reply raised more than a few chuckles. It was perfectly simple, but nonetheless quite true: 'Well it's really quite simple, you see I'm called Monty as well you know.' Montgomery left without making much of an impression, but perhaps the real reason why he was neither cheered nor applauded for his words of encouragement was that the soldiers understood only too well that Special Forces were never his particular favourites, although he was not averse to using their skills whenever the need arose.

Chapter IV

Another Step Closer

The Squadron, with an overall strength of eighteen officers and 262 other ranks, boarded their ships on 1 July 1943 and set sail for Port Said where they spent another three days making some last minute preparations and adjustments before taking part in further training exercises.

On 5 July preparations were finally complete and the Squadron embarked on what would be the start of the invasion of mainland Europe. Mayne and his small band of raiders formed only a fraction of what was numerically the largest amphibious assault of the war in terms of initial assault strength. The huge force comprised General Patton's Seventh US Army and General Montgomery's Eighth Army. Altogether the operation had a total strength of nearly half a million men in eight divisions. They would be transported in a vast convoy of over 3,200 ships of all shapes and sizes while some 4,000 British and American aircraft had been assembled to provide air cover for them.

The strength of Axis forces ranged against them on the island of Sicily had been estimated to be somewhere in the region of 400,000 soldiers. The bulk of the men were from five Italian infantry and five Italian coastal divisions. Their ranks had also been strengthened by the deployment of a further two German divisions, Hermann Göring Jäger and 15th Panzer.

At the time of the formation of the massive invasion fleet the majority of ordinary soldiers still did not know exactly where, or even what, their intended target was to be. That was rectified shortly after putting to sea when copies of a small booklet called *The Soldier's Guide to Sicily* were handed out. Having read quickly through its pages they were then able to make a very good educated guess. However guesswork was removed from the equation as intense briefings soon followed. It was hard work but by 9 July every single member of the Squadron, regardless of rank, had been made totally aware of his allocated task and of what was expected of him. Nothing would be left to chance as soldiers spent long hours studying and analysing the intelligence reports, maps, scale models and aerial photographs that had been brought on board just before setting sail.

The first action that the squadron was to undertake was part of Operation HUSKY, the code name assigned by the Allies to the invasion of Sicily. The landings were to take place along a hundred-mile stretch of coastline between the villages of Gela and Licata and would also extend up to Cassible, a few miles south of the historic port of Syracuse. The island of Sicily is the largest in the Mediterranean and covers roughly 10,000 square miles in area with a coastline of 600 miles. A large coastal defence battery had been sited at Capo-Murro-di-Porco, or in English the cape of the pig's nose. The gun emplacements situated there had been identified by intelligence sources as posing an unacceptable threat to the incoming invasion fleet. The men of the SRS were initially tasked with capturing and destroying the enemy gun battery while any further actions deemed necessary would be left to the discretion of their Commanding Officer, Major R.B. Mayne DSO.

Despite the fact that a large number of the men were hardened veterans and used to going into battle, many would be taking part in their first seaborne landing. Waiting to go into action was always the hardest part and the soldiers would have been feeling very tense and anxious for everything to get underway. Paddy Mayne made a point of moving between the various assembly points on the ship to visit all his waiting men and possibly ease some of their fears. To some his actions may have even seemed cheerful as he stopped and had a brief word with each of them before wishing them all the very best of luck. But behind the outward calmness he would have been just as keen as anyone to get things started. That brief interlude allowed him the time to say his own personal and private goodbyes to some of his closest companions. A large majority of the men assembled around him were his friends as well as his soldiers. He obviously knew and understood what some of their thoughts and worries would be as he had first-hand knowledge of such operations. During the early part of June 1941 he had taken part in the actions against the Vichy French at the Litani river in Syria as a young lieutenant with No.11 (Scottish) Commando. The section he commanded had been part of the unit known as Layforce under Colonel Bob Laycock.

During some of the heaviest fighting he had shown his true colours under fire and also gave a brief glimpse of what the future held as he was mentioned in despatches for his conduct, skill and courage.

Shortly after he had finished making his rounds the ship's loudspeaker system crackled into life with the much awaited but nonetheless ominous command: 'SRS, Embark.'

Fifteen minutes after midnight on 10 July 1943 the Special Raiding Squadron sprang swiftly into action and began disembarking from their two mother ships, *Ulster Monarch* and HMS *Dunera*. They would be loaded into nine landing craft, six of which would leave from the safety and comfort of the *Monarch* and three, one of them carrying the men of Alex Muirhead's Mortar Platoon, from *Dunera*.

The weather conditions encountered during the landings were atrocious with the strong winds, at times, exceeding force seven, which meant speeds of over 40 mph. The seas were whipped into a frenzy that in turn caused mountainous waves. In fact they had been so severe that earlier in the day it had been feared that the landings might either have to be postponed or aborted completely. The ships were totally blacked out except for the red glow from the invasion lamps as the men boarded their small craft. There were two very important reasons for the blackout: no lights could be seen by the island's defenders and the men's night vision would not be impaired so that they would find it much easier to accustom their eyes to the darkness of the prevailing conditions. The assault craft were suspended over the side of the *Monarch* by davits and some sections had to board them by crossing a plank placed precariously between the two craft. While making this dangerous transfer, Frank Josling slipped and lost his footing when a heavy surge hit the ship. The sudden movement caused the plank to slew dangerously to one side. It all happened so quickly that he was given no chance to save himself and plunged straight down into the boiling sea. Severely hampered by the sheer weight of all the kit that he was carrying, he began to sink like a stone. At that point he must have felt that surely a watery grave was to be the end for him. But Frank, who had originally been a commando, was made of sterner stuff and his quick wits and courage undoubtedly saved his life. The hard lessons drilled into him during training took over almost immediately as he held his breath, along with his nerve. Even while sinking he freed himself from his webbing and kicked out for the surface. Luck was certainly on his side as he broke through the surface and, despite the dreadful conditions, was quickly spotted and dragged back on board. He had been doubly lucky because he had also somehow avoided being crushed when he surfaced between the hull of the ship and the landing craft. Somehow, Josling had managed to escape drowning but he did not escape the razor-sharp wit of the men who were helping him. As he was being pulled out of the water he was met with a very unsympathetic greeting: 'Come on Frank hurry up, you'll not get out of this one so easily' was the sarcastic remark hurled at him. 'But hold on boys can't you see that I've lost all of my kit and my weapon' was his rather sheepish reply. Soaked through to the skin, dripping wet and shivering violently from the cold, he was hurriedly handed a replacement rifle and told to carry on. The remarks from his rescuers were not intended to be cruel or heartless since that type of banter was commonplace amongst them. But they knew that Frank could not be allowed to think too much about his close shave.

The members of C Section had also started to board their landing craft via an oiling door lower down in the ship's side. Boarding from that precarious position in rough seas was literally a leap in the dark for them. A young naval officer had been stationed beside the door to tell the men when he felt that it was safe for them to make their jump. *Monarch* was rolling and lurching heavily from side to side in the rough seas and it must have been a hugely daunting task even to contemplate making any sort of move as the landing craft were also swaying about as the ship moved. The latter could be at least three feet away from the side of the ship on one roll and then over six feet away on the next. That meant that the timing for their jumps was of the utmost importance and had to be just right.

Sid Payne stood and waited anxiously for his turn; the fourth in line, he had watched three successful jumps. Sid got the timing for his leap just about right and managed to land on top of the side of his landing craft. He was very thankful that the men already on board were able to get a firm grip on him and drag him down onto the floor of the boat. Suddenly from somewhere just behind him he heard a rather muffled but very urgent scream for help. Standing behind him in the line had been Private Ernie Smith and the timing of his jump had not been very good at all. He was desperately clinging on to the edge of the landing craft like grim death. Smith needed all the strength that he could possibly muster as his grip was extremely tenuous. The weight of the kit on his back was threatening to loosen his hold and pull him downwards. Luckily for him, Sid Payne had heard his cry for help above the crash of the waves and, along with the other soldiers, managed to manhandle him over the side.

Elsewhere on the *Monarch* things were not going completely to plan either as the davits holding one of the other landing craft had jammed solid and the damaged mechanism would not release it. Sheer brute force and strength had to be applied but it still took several minutes of hard work and hammering to free them. Another craft was put out of action when the davits smashed the winches that raised and lowered its armoured door. Luckily the Navy was able to produce another one from somewhere and the soldiers quickly transferred into it. The worsening weather and sea conditions were causing grave concerns about the risk of damage to the small boats. Those concerns forced a rethink and new orders were given to the naval crews who were told to cast off and make their way to the protected side of the ship where it was hoped that the embarkation could continue. That decision proved to be the right one and allowed the remainder of the Squadron safely to complete their transfers.

With all the men and equipment loaded the next phase of the landings could begin. Navigation in such treacherous conditions was very difficult but, thankfully, a naval gunboat had been sent in to patrol the waters just offshore. The boat's officers were forced to use loudhailers to make their orders heard above the noise of the howling wind but this was effective and some of the LCAs followed their directions and made it safely inshore. A British submarine which had surfaced recently proved to be yet another unforeseen and hazardous obstacle to the landings. In the darkness one of the Squadron's craft came to an abrupt halt when it crashed into her hull. For a few breathtaking moments everything stopped as the startled occupants stared upwards in disbelief. They felt sure that it had to be a German U-boat and that their war was over even before it had really started. The submarine had been showing only a small blue light and this may have been mistaken as a signal from the shore parties who were trying to guide them in. Thankfully for all concerned their relief was almost instantaneous when they heard some very sharp four-letter words being exchanged between the opposing seamen in broad English accents. That particular submarine was one of seven which had been detailed to lie off the coast to act as beacons and guide the task force on to the release points off the beaches.

As they made their final run into the landing areas the men began to tense up as they watched the beams from the searchlights playing back and forth across the water. They realised that they were helpless spectators and wondered if they would be spotted. Many also stared upwards into the darkness of the night sky and watched as yet more searchlights followed the noise made by Royal Air Force bombers flying overhead. The aircraft had been sent in to do a softening up job on the coastal defences prior to the landings. Earlier during the day the United States Army Air Force had also sent some of its heavy bombers over to attempt to destroy the Axis headquarters and the telegraphic centre that the Italians had located at Taormina.

The weather conditions were also having a devastating and adverse effect on the armada of gliders carrying the troops and equipment destined for other targets on Sicily. But perhaps the two main causes of failure for the operation were the lack of training and the inexperience of the American crews manning the Douglas C-47

Skytrains being used to tow the gliders. (The C-47 was known as the Dakota in RAF service, which became the name by which the aircraft is best known but the USAAF retained the name Skytrain.) Sadly they made a shambles of the timings for the release of their towing lines with some gliders being released far too early or far short of their various landing zones while others were cast off in the wrong place. The gliders and more especially their fragile human cargoes found themselves having to pay a very costly price for those obviously avoidable mistakes. Operation HUSKY had been planned to include four separate airborne elements, two British and two American, each with its own tasks. The British tasks had been assigned the code name Operation LADBROKE and were to be undertaken by men of 1st Bn, Border Regiment, 2nd Bn, South Staffordshire Regiment and 9th Field Company, Royal Engineers. Those three units formed 1 Air Landing Brigade and were under orders to land below the town of Syracuse, which lay on a bay on the south-east coast. The South Staffs were to capture and hold the Ponte Grande Bridge to the south of the town and spanning the Anapo river. It was seen as being vitally important to the overall success of the operation. The men of the Border Regiment were to push forward and make their way down into the town of Syracuse. Once that objective had been achieved it was hoped that they could hold onto their positions until they were relieved by units from 5th Division. It had been planned that if everything went well this would take place some time during the following day. The men, along with all their personal equipment and weapons, had been loaded into 137 Waco Hadrian and ten Airspeed Horsa glid-ers. Sadly, as events began to unfold, things soon started to go terribly wrong for them. Of the original 147 gliders that set out, two were shot down by ground fire, one landed in Malta, ten landed back in Tunisia, North Africa, sixty-nine crash landed into the sea, resulting in the deaths of 252 men, while the remainder were scattered over the area between Capo Passero and Capo-Murro-di-Porco. Only twenty managed to land on the island of Sicily. And it owed more to good luck than good judgement that they were anywhere near their designated landing areas. A total of eleven officers and 191 other ranks had actually made it onto dry land.

Those men who did reach Sicily found their landings to be extremely rough and, sadly, many were either killed or suffered severe wounds from being crushed badly when they hit the ground. Whoever had been responsible for conducting the forward planning in regard to the landing zones had either totally failed to realise, or just did not take into account that due to the small fields, hills, terraces and countless dry-stone walls it was definitely not ideal country on which to try to land gliders. But the soldiers on board the gliders who had been forced to ditch in the sea faced an even worse fate. It must have seemed as if they were going to be rescued when they heard the sounds of landing craft approaching them. But it was not to be; they were doomed and for most of those brave men the engines would be the last noise that they heard. The Squadron had their primary objective in sight and were on very tight timings. There was no other choice but to push on towards the beach. The soldiers from the downed gliders were getting desperate and as the LCAs passed by them the occupants could hear many calling out 'have a heart, mates'. The terrible sounds of those men in obvious distress must have had a dreadful effect on everyone on board the landing craft. But perhaps they weighed heaviest on Paddy Mayne as he valued every single life very highly. His men knew that he would have died himself rather than risk another man's life for no obvious reason or gain. In fact, he did remember having to make the terrible decision to abandon those poor men as he mentioned it later in a letter to a friend: 'It was a terrible thing to have to do'. However, some were lucky enough to be picked up and rescued from that terrible fate, including Brigadier Phillip Hicks, Colonel George Chatterton and the men from his glider, No.2. They had supposedly been hit and shot down by heavy enemy flak but there is strong evidence to suggest that they, with many others of the glider force, were shot down by 'blue-on-blue' or, as it is known today, 'friendly fire'. Once Brigadier Hicks and his men, who by that time had lost most of their equipment and weapons, reached the beach they joined up with about 150 other men who had also been lucky enough to make it ashore. In total the casualties suffered by 1 Air Landing Brigade and the Glider Pilot Regiment were given as 605 men of which, sadly, over 300 lost their lives through drowning. Brigadier Hicks was later to command the Air Landing Brigade that saw action at Arnhem. Colonel Chatterton became the Commanding Officer of the Glider Pilot Regiment during D-Day, Arnhem and eventually the Rhine crossing.

As the landing craft made their final approaches towards the beach they reduced their speed to almost a crawl and through the wet and murky conditions the soldiers were just about able to make out the dark outline of Sicily. Private Jack Nixon, a member of No.3 Troop, had been landed on the island two days earlier from a destroyer along with five other men from the COPPs (Combined Operations Pilotage Parties). Due to the poor standards of the defending Italian soldiers they had managed easily to keep their presence hidden. That allowed them a certain degree of confidence when they signalled vital information about the landing conditions out to the submarine lying offshore. Once that information had been received and processed it was then sent on to the higher commands for their careful consideration. Jack was anxiously lying in wait on a small sandy cove and flashing his torch to guide the men into their designated landing areas. By 3.15 a.m. the entire Squadron had landed successfully on the beach and moved quickly up to the sharp outcrops of rocks that formed the base of the cliffs. They found it extremely hard to believe that no land mines had been laid around the landing sites. It was also strangely quiet and not a single shot had been fired at them. However, those things were unexpected bonuses that no one was ever going to complain about.

Chapter V

Into Action

Every troop and section had made it ashore safely and there had been no reports of any casualties. Intelligence reports had indicated that, at one point on the cliff face, they would find an extremely steep and very difficult climb. But they were greeted with yet another bonus, as the Italian soldiers stationed at the coastal defences had been good enough to provide them with some steps, which the kind-hearted defenders had carved into the rock face to provide themselves with easy access to the small beach.

As Jack Nixon made his way up those steps he passed a very young and frightened Italian soldier who appeared to be totally petrified. 'The poor wee boy was standing ashen faced and rigidly at attention. Perhaps it was out of terror, surprise or just sheer luck that he made no challenge to us as we approached him.' His total lack of movement almost certainly saved his life as it meant that he was left standing there as the raiders filed upwards and past him. Had he been brave enough to make one wrong move it surely would have been his last. Alex Muirhead brought his 3-inch mortar platoon into action immediately and began a heavy bombardment of the enemy positions. Private George Bass had the honour of firing the Squadron's first round of the engagement, a phosphorous/smoke round that was normally fired for sighting purposes. Bass's hands were cold and slightly wet and he was also feeling quite anxious as he prepared to drop that first round into the mortar tube. However, he need not have worried: fortune must surely favour the brave as it landed in the middle of the main cordite dump for the gun battery and ignited it. The blast, and the intense heat generated by the round, caused a tremendous explosion. It also started some very large and extensive fires that lit up the night sky. As the sections spread out and began making their way towards their various objectives contact was finally made with the Italian defenders. Red and green trails from tracer rounds started to flash across the dark sky in all directions and the sound of heavy bursts of small-arms fire filled the air.

As well as the main objective, the coastal battery with its barracks and underground bunkers, earlier intelligence reports had pinpointed a heavily defended farmhouse, known locally as Damerio, that would have to be dealt with. Lieutenant John Wiseman, who commanded one of the leading sections, used the covering fire provided by the Squadron's mortars to make up some extra ground. He moved his section up to, and through, the coils of barbed wire that formed part of the perimeter defences. On reaching the wire he ordered his men to take cover while they waited for a short break in the bombardment. At the first opportunity he moved his section forward and they charged at breakneck speed into the gun position.

With the element of total surprise on their side they were able to kill, capture or wound the forty enemy soldiers who were taking shelter inside. Many had felt sure that the Italians would put up a much stiffer resistance in defence of their home soil. During an earlier conversation Paddy Mayne and Reg Seekings had discussed the use of bayonets during the attacks. Both agreed that it could be a valuable tactic and so Seekings had ordered his men to fix their bayonets. He also made a specific point of telling them not to hold back and to go in as hard as they possibly could. They put in such a ferocious attack on the command post and barrack blocks complex that bullets were very nearly secondary since the defenders almost died of fright at the sight of cold steel. The raiders' fierce charge forced the inhabitants, who turned out to be a sorry mixture of middle-aged soldiers and pitiful looking civilians, to try to flee for their lives in absolute terror.

While that attack was taking place the men of No.1 Troop were coming under increasingly heavy fire from a fortified machine-gun emplacement. Private Nobby Noble recognised the danger of the situation and reacted immediately by opening up with some heavy bursts from his Bren. The accuracy and fierce rate of fire that he was able to lay down on the enemy position had a devastating effect. He succeeded in putting the enemy machine gun completely out of action and also killed twelve Italian soldiers in the process. By silencing the gun so quickly he almost certainly saved lives and cleared the way forward. Lance-Sergeant Shaw was also engaged very heavily in the ferocious attack on the battery. He lobbed a hand grenade at the enemy positions but, unfortunately for all his comrades around him, it somehow failed to find its intended target. It struck one of the concrete walls of the bunker and bounced straight back towards them. It exploded on the spot where his men had been standing just a few seconds before. However, this did not cause any great anxiety or panic among the men who accepted it and carried on with their attack although, as usual, they made a point later of reminding him of what had happened. Terry Moore came to his rescue by making a valid comment in his defence: 'Well things like that happen all the time during the confusion of an attack and you really never knew what was around the next corner anyway'.

Another close call occurred as Lance-Corporal Ginger Hodgkinson was making his way cautiously around the side of a gun emplacement. Suddenly he found himself confronted with the sight of some very heavily armed men coming menacingly towards him out of the darkness. Although he was slightly off balance and had been taken by surprise his reactions to the danger that faced him were immediate. Without thinking he instantly brought his Bren gun up to the hip and squeezed hard on the trigger. The Bren was a notorious weapon for rearing upwards when fired on automatic and the tracer rounds zipped harmlessly upwards into the dark sky. Perhaps it was caused by the sudden shock, a loose grip in the wet slippery conditions, or a combination of both, but either way Sid Payne was a very thankful man as he breathed a deep sigh of relief. He had been the leading man of his section as they had started putting in their attack on the same enemy gun emplacement.

The men from No.3 Troop were sent forward to attack the Damerio farmhouse, and to provide covering fire for some of the men from Nos 1 and 2 Troops. That particular

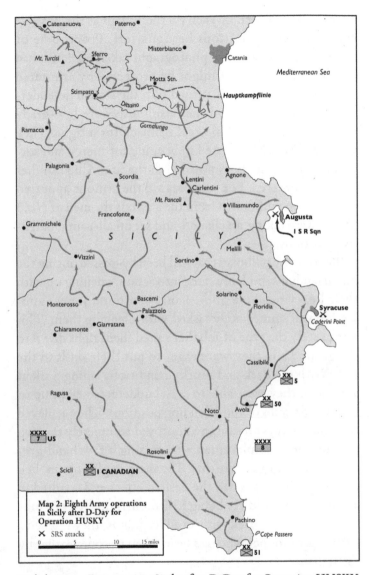

Eighth Army Operations in Sicily after D-Day for Operation HUSKY

farmhouse had been marked on their maps as the possible site of a communications headquarters. From some of the aerial reconnaissance photographs taken earlier, it had also been noted that it might be protected by armoured vehicles. However, as it turned out, the Italian defenders stationed in and around the farmhouse were low-grade infantry soldiers with no real stomach for a fight. They were really only interested in begging for mercy and surrendering as quickly as possible to the first Allied soldier they encountered. For some reason the armour appeared to have been withdrawn from the area but the men of No.3 Troop were taking no chances and set up all-round defensive positions.

Two enemy pillboxes that had been by-passed during the initial landings suddenly came into action, opening up with their heavy machine guns. Lance-Corporal Jones's sub-section was immediately tasked with silencing them. This was exactly the type of job that suited them right down to the ground and they were eager to put their skills to the test. With the dark and murky conditions aiding a silent approach, they were able to crawl undetected right up to the outside walls of the offending positions. They achieved their objective with ease and destroyed completely the two machine-gun emplacements by tossing a few hand grenades in through the fire slits. The sharp explosions in such confined conditions had the desired effect and resulted in all the enemy soldiers being killed outright. Jones's sub-section also came back with an added bonus; they rescued a British paratrooper who had been taken prisoner earlier by the Italians.

By 5.00 a.m. it was less than two hours after the landings and the coastal defence battery had been successfully captured and destroyed by demolition charges set by the Sappers who had landed with the Squadron. Lieutenant Derrick Harrison was a happy and relieved man after watching the destruction as it had been his task to ensure that the Sappers arrived safely and carried out their very important job. Shortly afterwards the other sections began to arrive at the Damerio farmhouse, which had been designated as the rendezvous point. As they started to re-group they brought with them an ever-increasing number of scared, sullen and bedraggled prisoners. Jack Nixon looked at the assembled mass of sad faces and suddenly remembered the young Italian sentry he had passed by a few hours earlier. He quickly made his way back to the cliffs and was amazed to find him still standing in exactly the same spot.

The sun had risen into the early morning sky and so, from their vantage point, the raiders were able to look down and watch the vast armada of ships and landing craft that, thanks in part to their efforts, could move safely inshore. Various theories exist regarding the ease with which the gun battery was taken: some state that it was due to the bombing carried out by the Royal Air Force, others that it was because the Italians, thinking it would be impossible for anyone to attack in such foul weather conditions, had simply put the lights out for the night and gone to sleep. However, the men landing on the beach would have had no prior knowledge of any of those facts. They had been given a job to do and had gone ahead and carried it out. The taking of the main objective meant that four 6-inch guns, three 20mm anti-aircraft guns, one range-finder and several heavy machine guns had been destroyed. Between fifty and sixty prisoners had been taken while a further fifty enemy soldiers were either killed or wounded in the actions.

So far operations had gone to plan and the objective had been thoroughly and satisfactorily dealt with. Mayne was undoubtedly in very high spirits. He was also extremely pleased with the performance of his soldiers and their outstanding results under fire. He had his feet firmly planted back on dry land and it was more than obvious to everyone around him that he was a man who was in total and absolute command of the entire situation. His soldiers had understandably been feeling slightly nervous and apprehensive at the start of the invasion but now all the niggling doubts and worries had been removed from the equation.

Mayne had spent a short period collecting his thoughts and mulling over the plus points and successes of the operation. He realised how well the mortar platoon had performed so he called for Lieutenant Muirhead to come forward and have a quick word with him in private. As usual he came straight to the point: 'Well done, do you want a medal or a promotion?' Alex Muirhead paused for a brief moment while he thought over the recent events and also considered the future. He then quite calmly and quietly replied: 'I'll take the promotion, Sir, if you don't mind as I am sure that my widow could do with the extra money' [Muirhead later went on to be awarded the Military Cross and a Mention in Despatches during campaigns with 1st SAS in North West Europe in 1944–5]. Mayne's expression never changed; he just stood very still and made no comment about the rather tongue-in-cheek reply. He would have known that the young man in front of him, together with the rest of his men, did not seek, or need, the glory of medals pinned to their chests. He was totally aware of the fact that 'men follow courage not rank'. The principal honour that every man in the regiment strove for was to be permitted to wear the famous wings on his left breast. That honour had to be earned the hard way and came only at the behest of their peers.

Chapter VI

Completion

At 6.00 a.m. another two coastal defence batteries opened up from positions farther inland and began firing their heavy shells towards the ships lying at anchor offshore. If these guns were not silenced they could inflict incredible damage. Mayne was not the type of officer who would stand still and rest on his laurels so he acted decisively and decided to launch an attack against them. The large number of captured Italian soldiers was, however, becoming a big problem for the Squadron. They could not be taken along with them nor could any men be spared to stay behind and stand guard over them. Mayne solved the troublesome situation when he left them all in the capable hands of the Brigadier and the rest of the rescued glider troops, much to their disgust.

The fleet began to respond to the fire from the inshore batteries with salvoes from their heavy guns. That return fire was causing serious problems to the advancing men as some shells were falling short. An immediate signal was sent to the fleet informing them of the Squadron's intentions and requesting that they cease firing at once. As the Squadron made its way up the Della Maddalena peninsula towards the gun batteries they came under constant sniper fire as well as heavier fire from the many farmhouses that were being defended heavily by the enemy. When moving forward, the raiders usually tried to have a Bren gunner placed out on the flanks of each troop. That would provide them with some good fields of fire while still allowing fire to be concentrated on the centre of the advance if needed.

Dougie Monteith had spotted a potential target so he hurriedly threw himself forward and brought his Bren tightly up into his shoulder. He stared down the barrel as he lined up an enemy soldier in his sights and began to tighten his finger on the trigger. But he stared in utter amazement at what happened next. He watched the top of the Italian's head suddenly disappear in a shower of flesh and blood as the tracer rounds hammered into it. What seemed even stranger was the fact that the virtually beheaded man continued moving forward for a short distance before collapsing. Monteith stood up and glanced quickly across to where he knew the shots had come from. He smiled inwardly and began moving forward again; Jack Nixon had once again shown his prowess with the Bren.

Under the direction of Major Mayne, the farmhouses were mopped up fairly easily as soon as they were encountered. The defenders turned out to be yet more Italian soldiers who soon came out with their hands raised in surrender. Sid Payne and a few men from C Section of No.1 Troop had been making their way cautiously across a field towards one of the occupied farmhouses.

We all had our weapons held at the ready and still had our bayonets fixed. But before putting in our attack we decided to take a short break and sample some of the local tomatoes. Everyone crouched down to eat while we rested our weapons against a stone wall. After having a short break we continued with the advance, but when we reached the building it was strangely empty. The general consensus of opinion was that the sight of our bayonets showing above the wall had simply been too much for the defenders.

The enemy soldiers holding one farmhouse emerged into the open and started frantically waving white flags at the approaching troops. Aware of what that action meant, a section moved forward quickly to round up yet another group of prisoners. Suddenly, from among the seemingly passive Italians, one opened fire with an automatic weapon on the unsuspecting section. Caught completely off guard, two men were hit and fell. Corporal Geoff Caton took the full force from the burst and dropped where he stood. Although stunned, the remainder of the section stormed forward immediately and ensured that no one else would carry out such an act of treachery. Tragically, Corporal Caton had been wounded mortally when the bullets hammered into his body around the groin area; he died a short time later.

One particular Italian soldier must have had no idea of what had occurred over the last few hours as he was spotted cycling happily towards the advancing Squadron with his rifle tied to the top tube of his bicycle. It was only when he got closer that he suddenly came to his senses and realised that he was about to make a grave and, possibly, fatal error.

He quickly turned around and began frantically to pedal back the way he had come. Lance-Corporal Bob Gallier was the first to react and brought his weapon to the shoulder to loose off a few rounds in the general direction of the rapidly disappearing Italian. One round hit the frame of the bike just below where it joined the saddle pillar. The seat post sheared off and the rider was dumped in a sorry heap on the ground. What happened next resembled something from a pantomime and took everyone completely by surprise, but Gallier in particular. With cries of 'Grazie, Grazie', Bob found himself being grabbed, kissed and hugged by a very emotional and extremely happy Italian who obviously felt that, instead of being shot and killed, some incredibly skilful shooting had just spared his miserable life. The men of the Raiding Squadron had little or no respect for the Italian soldiers as they had fought against them throughout the desert campaigns where they had witnessed how local people and prisoners of war had been treated and suffered at the hands of Mussolini's troops.

Despite having left a great number of prisoners behind it was inevitable that the farther inland they proceeded the more the Squadron collected. Sid Payne was walking along in front of a group of newly captured prisoners when he got the shock of his life. Although wary of them he was not paying attention to any particular individual. Suddenly one of them stepped out in front of him and said in a rather strong English voice, 'Hello, Sid'. Much to his surprise that particular 'prisoner' turned out to be an airborne soldier who had been one of his old mates from the South Staffordshires.

On most occasions incoming fire from enemy machine-gun positions could be fairly easy to spot and deal with, but the deadly threat to the Squadron from the sniper's rifle was increasing steadily. Private Alex Skinner had been hit and wounded in the leg and hips during the initial actions and was beginning to suffer severe pains from his wounds. However, that did not deter him as he decided to take matters into his own hands and do something about the snipers. While the rest of his comrades were involved in the attack on and capture of one of the farmhouses, called Massa Alacona, he managed to spot the concealed positions which the snipers were using as firing points. He moved out very slowly and cautiously towards them. The area of ground that he had to cross to get within rifle range was rock hard, with very sparse growth and provided little or no cover to use for protection. Despite those problems, Skinner managed to get close enough to deal with them. He waited and watched for any telltale signs, the slightest movement, smoke or a muzzle flash. Then, one by one, he got them into the cross hairs of his sights and put them permanently out of action. The long hours of target practice on the rifle range paid off and in relatively quick succession he had accounted for three snipers. The levels of fighting and resistance encountered continued to be short and sharp as the various sections made their way towards the gun emplacements.

As the Squadron continued to advance farther inland yet more snipers began to open up from their concealed locations. It was Private John 'Nobby' Noble who next took the initiative as he had been one of the first to spot a few of their firing positions. Once again, as with Private Skinner before him, neither his own safety nor the danger of being shot even entered his mind. The snipers were causing some serious problems to his mates and they simply had to be dealt with. Noble's selfless action was decisive and even more successful. Without any doubt, he had saved many lives as he accounted for a further eight of the troublesome snipers.

While the sections made their way across the peninsula many more groups of airborne troops who had decided to lie up and wait for help were discovered. They had failed to take the bridge at Syracuse and some gave the Squadron more problems than the Italian defenders as they mistakenly kept opening fire on them. A few of these misplaced Allied troops turned out to be a small group of Canadian soldiers who had also lost their bearings. They were quickly updated on the fast changing situation and pointed in the right direction. All the sections finally reached the outskirts of the battery and began to take up attacking positions surrounding the emplacement.

Mayne was where he was always to be found, right in the thick of things. He was tireless as he directed and controlled the actions of his men. Private Monteith was making his way forward while trying to find a good position from which to lay down covering fire from his Bren gun. Suddenly, out of the blue, he heard a rather stern and very familiar loud voice barking a command at him: 'Get down'. He immediately stopped in his tracks and looked up. 'Paddy Mayne was standing up and walking about in plain view of everyone just about ten yards from where I was lying. His pistol was still in its holster and he was waving his officer's cane about as if conducting some sort of orchestra.' The advice given to Monteith took the form of a very simple but true statement: 'Be careful and keep your head down laddie, as you'll be no good to me with a hole in it'.

Sergeant-Major Rose was another who had good reason to be thankful for the alertness of his commanding officer as two well-placed rounds from Mayne's Colt .45 killed an Italian soldier who had been just about to shoot the warrant officer in the back. There was no admonition in his voice. 'Be careful Mister Rose' was the only comment heard from Mayne. Under the deadly and accurate covering fire provided for them by Alex Muirhead's Mortar Platoon, Nos 1 and 2 Troops began to put in their joint attacks. Forward movement was proving difficult as they were being met with some very strong and concentrated resistance. No.1 Troop at that point was being hampered badly and held back by a heavy barrage of fire directed at them from an enemy pillbox.

The sub-section under Sergeant Reg Seekings was also suffering badly from the same fire and had been pinned down. They faced a further serious threat from some accurate and deadly mortar fire. Seekings, although only lightly armed with a few hand grenades and a revolver, decided that it was time to put the offending pillbox out of action. He ordered his men to move out onto the flank of the enemy gun emplacements. Showing total disregard for the constant hail of machine-gun bullets and mortar fire being thrown at them, they rushed headlong towards the enemy positions. The ferocity and speed of their attack was stunning and utterly successful. They overran the pillbox and killed all the enemy soldiers who had been manning it. With the threat from the offending pillbox eliminated, they turned their attention towards the mortars. Nothing, or no one, was going to stop them or stand in their way as they stormed forward and into the midst of the mortar crews. Once again the resistance of the defenders was simply brushed aside and the mortars put out of action as well. Lance-Corporal Dalziel, with another sub-section, had also been sent forward and tasked specifically to out-flank the enemy positions from the left. Despite the fact that they were clearly, and dangerously, outnumbered they still managed to kill or rout a very substantial number of enemy soldiers.

These two decisive actions helped clear the way forward and made it possible for the men of No.1 Troop to join in the final charge into the battery. Along with No.2 Troop, which was being led by Captain Harry Poat, they succeeded finally in killing or capturing sixty enemy soldiers as well as taking the battery itself. On closer inspection it was found that some of the enemy guns had never even opened fire. There were still a few pockets of enemy resistance to be dealt with and the 3-inch mortars again opened fire. Once more they were successful as they set a large ammunition magazine on fire. The fierce fires eventually caused the ammunition to explode. At the same time, No.1 Troop attacked and captured another two enemy gun emplacements. The enemy soldiers manning the last few remaining positions knew that they had been well beaten. Any further thoughts of resistance had been thoroughly knocked out of the Italian defenders and the fighting was over.

The doors to the abandoned food store of the last gun battery captured were thrown open and the prisoners along with the rescued airborne troops joined the men of the Squadron for a much needed and well-deserved break-fast. It was fairly obvious to see that they were overjoyed at the thought of having some real food to put in their stom-achs for a change. That was possibly due to the fact that they had been totally sickened, and in some cases turned a strange shade of red, by the tomatoes that they had picked from the many fields and stuffed into themselves during their journey down the island.

At 4.00 p.m. the Squadron left Alacona farm and set off down the main road towards the port of Syracuse. As the men made their way down they once again met small pockets of resistance from snipers and more defended farms. But as each little remnant of the defeated enemy was encountered it was attacked and dealt with swiftly. The Squadron's soldiers spent the night resting and gathering their thoughts at one of the many farms that they had captured and in the morning they met up with the forward elements of 5th Division who were on the road into Syracuse. Thankfully, they were able to hand over all their prisoners, who by then numbered over 500. A very proud Major Mayne decided that because his men were known as the Special Raiding Squadron, and were not just some run-of-the-mill unit, they should march in four ranks instead of the normal three used by the Army. (Ranks of four had been the normal drill until 1937 when each infantry company was reduced from four to three platoons and each platoon from four to three sections.) As they marched down into Syracuse they crossed the bridge that the airborne troops had been tasked to capture. It was fairly obvious that some very heavy and costly fighting had taken place around it. Thankfully it remained intact and it seemed that no attempt had been made to demolish it. The broken and shattered remains of three gliders and much of their contents were strewn about the ground. The soldiers who had the misfortune of being transported in them referred to them as 'flying coffins', as they were very flimsy and offered little or no protection. This was due to the fact that they were constructed mostly from wood and covered with a thin layer of fabric.

As Bob McDougall neared the end of the bridge, he stopped and stared with sheer disbelief at the gruesome sight that met his eyes. The charred remains of three soldiers were still in position behind their machine gun. They had obviously suffered an almost indescribable death. Their bodies had been literally cremated as the Germans had used flamethrowers on them. That was the first time that McDougall had seen the results of that weapon and he honestly hoped that it would be the last. A lone German bomber suddenly appeared flying very low overhead. It became obvious that it had spotted them when it turned around and came in for an attack. The diving plane released a bomb that looked almost certain to land smack in the middle of the marching men. Major Mayne who as usual was at the front of the Squadron neither blinked an eye nor changed stride. Only one man broke ranks to dive for the cover of a nearby ditch as the bomb dropped harmlessly over their heads and into a field where it exploded. Despite the fact that he was a regular soldier and also a very well liked member of the squadron he was told to pack his kit and return to his parent unit. Some may regard this particular incident as foolish or just a show of bravado on Mayne's part but it was neither. The RTU'ing of the soldier who dived for cover could also be said to be extremely harsh but it best describes the attitude required from those who served with the Special Air Service. It was imperative that they were able to depend completely on the men serving alongside them in all situations and conditions, no matter how deadly or serious these might be.

On 12 July the Squadron was ferried back to *Ulster Monarch*, which was lying at anchor in the harbour. This brought to a very successful end the first operation under the new title. After a somewhat shaky start due to the adverse weather conditions, the Capo-Murro-di-Porco and Syracuse operations had been a total success as far as the men of Special Raiding Squadron were concerned. Overall, they had captured or destroyed eighteen large guns, four mortars, three rangefinders and numerous heavy machine guns and small arms and had taken the surrender of over 500 prisoners and either killed or wounded about 200 enemy soldiers. The losses incurred by the Squadron were light: in addition to the death of Corporal Caton, two men were wounded during the actions: Privates A Allen and H Hill. Private Allen received his wounds in the same action that saw the loss of Corporal Geoff Caton. Although he survived his injuries, they were so severe that after treatment he was no longer able to continue soldiering and was demobbed from the armed services. (Although Private Alex Skinner had also been wounded he did not report his injuries to the Medical Officer lest he be refused permission to take part in further operations.) Material losses in the Squadron totalled one rifle, two berets and one water bottle.

Also included in the Squadron's official reports of the actions, dated 11 July 1943, was the capture of fifty 'gallini' with their 'normal complement'. It was only later, when the report had travelled farther along the chain of command to reach the staff officers, was it realised that what really had been captured was fifty chickens and their eggs. The men of the SAS never missed the slightest chance of poking fun at, or having a good laugh at the expense of, their superior or senior ranks. Those who compiled the report must have considered that the capture of fifty 'gallini' would have looked very impressive to those people reading the reports. Was there a round of backslapping before the truth was uncovered?

The Squadron's night's sleep on board the *Monarch* was rudely interrupted when German and Italian planes mounted a very heavy and concentrated bombing raid on the harbour. George Bass was one of the many men watching the battle between the aircraft and the shore batteries that night. 'It was an awesome sight, more like something resembling a huge fireworks display. There were shells of every type bursting all around us and tracer rounds flying everywhere across the night sky.' The defences had not yet been established fully and no searchlights were in position so all the anti-aircraft guns, both on board the ships and on land, were told to open fire with everything they had. Alex Muirhead remembered vividly that they were all watching that intense gunfire display from under the shelter of a covered deck.

> Paddy Mayne was a very angry man indeed at his sleep being so rudely disturbed. He was up on the open deck just pacing about and shaking his huge fist at the night sky. The shrapnel was raining down on him but he took no notice of it, he wasn't hit at all. Why I just do not know.

What Muirhead and others did not know was that an air raid was one thing that did frighten Mayne. During Eighth Army's advance the previous winter he had overnighted near Benghazi with his friend Major Jack

Christie of 6 LAA Battery but his sleep had been disturbed by an air raid on Benghazi harbour and Mayne made a speedy exit in the morning telling Christie that he had no idea how anybody could take this kind of soldiering. As Mayne was commissioned originally in the Royal Artillery, and into a light AA battery, it is perhaps as well that he did not pursue that avenue of soldiering. (On commissioning Mayne was posted to 5 LAA Battery, based in Newtownards and north Down; the battery was part of 8th AA Regiment RA (SR) (later 8th (Belfast) HAA Regiment RA (SR)).)

Major R.B. Mayne was awarded a Bar to his DSO, the citation for which reads:

On July 10th 1943 & 12th July 1943 Major R.B. Mayne carried out two successful operations. The first, the capture and destruction of a C.D. battery on Capo-Murro-di-Porco, the outcome of which was vital to the safe landing of XIII Corps. By nightfall 10/7/43 S.R.S. had captured three additional Btys, 450 prisoners as well as killing 200/300 Italians. The second operation was the capture and holding of the town of Augusta. The landing was carried out in daylight, a most hazardous combined operation. By the audacity displayed, the Italians were forced from their positions and masses of valuable stores and equipment were saved from enemy destruction. In both of these operations it was Major Mayne's courage, determination and superb leadership, which proved the key to success. He personally led his men from the landing craft in the face of heavy machine gun fire. By this action, he succeeded in forcing his way to ground where it was possible to form up and sum up the enemy's defences.

Captain Harry Poat and Lieutenant John Wiseman were each awarded the Military Cross; Sergeant Seekings was awarded the DCM; Lance-Corporal Dalziel, Lance-Corporal Jones, Privates Nobel and Skinner were all awarded the Military Medal.

The actions that led to the capture and subsequent destruction of the gun batteries and installations at Capo-Murro-di-Porco and Syracuse had lasted for some seventeen hours and covered a distance of over twenty-four miles. Throughout their dangerous journey inland the men of the Special Raiding Squadron had been outnumbered on most occasions by at least fifty to one.

Chapter VII

Augusta: Daylight Operation

The Squadron's members now found themselves safely back on board one of their two original mother ships. It was fairly crowded and space was at a premium throughout *Ulster Monarch* as some wounded soldiers had been ferried out from the island to receive treatment. The raiders, despite being physically and mentally exhausted, were looking forward to a rest. Messages of congratulations from the top brass as well as their own officers were doing the rounds and, naturally, everyone felt elated at a job well done. The vessel was a hive of noise and activity as their spirits were obviously still very high and adrenalin was still flowing freely. The soldiers were tending to basic and essential needs: eating, sorting out kit, having showers and exchanging stories about the last two days' actions. Some close calls were remembered and good shooting praised, while a few mistakes were recalled and those who had made them subjected to the usual cruel banter and laughter.

But rest and recreation were not to be the next items on the agenda as new, and urgent, orders had just arrived from General Dempsey about the task that he now wanted the Squadron to undertake. Word was quickly passed around the ship that Major Mayne was about to call a conference. He felt that it would be necessary not only to make plans for the operation but also to determine exactly what would be expected from his men and, with some of his fellow senior officers, he began studying the latest maps and aerial photographs. The time allowed for any planning was very limited which meant that the session had to be of a very exact nature and kept extremely brief. This would be a rare break from normal procedure as Paddy Mayne had always been a very thorough planner and did not like any detail, however small it might have appeared, left to chance.

The assembled soldiers realised very quickly that their next operation was to be yet another frontal assault from their small landing craft. However, the added danger to the Squadron was that this time they were going to be used in a daylight raid: to capture and hold the Italian naval base at the port of Augusta. Once in overall control they had to ensure that there was absolutely no chance of any unnecessary damage or demolition occurring to the vital harbour installations. The town had then to be entered, cleared of opposition and made secure. Reports gathered from intelligence sources stated that Augusta was being used by the *Kriegsmarine* as a re-supply depot for their submarines and E-boats based in the Mediterranean. It also had the ominous reputation of being one of the best-maintained and defended ports on Sicily.

The formidable fortifications included reinforced concrete bunkers, blockhouses and fortified emplacements for the heavy coastal defence guns. The heavier guns would also be supported by the usual array of light anti-aircraft guns and a substantial number of machine guns of all calibres. These defensive positions were all linked by a series of tunnels and the latest intelligence reports indicated that this was a very heavily garrisoned base. Crack German troops from the Hermann Göring Panzer Division were also rumoured to be stationed at Augusta; it was believed that they had been sent there to add extra support to the Italian troops. Someone had to be the bearer of the bad tidings and so Derrick Harrison was given the thankless job of telling the soldiers their rest was about to be rudely interrupted. Perhaps it was because he was always seen to be smiling, had a very pleasant disposition and was well liked – and known in the ranks as 'Happy Harry' – that he was chosen. Perhaps it was just that he had been the closest junior officer but his task turned out to be much easier than he had first thought and he was given the strange feeling that, as most soldiers do, they had already got wind that something was about to happen. On hearing the news they subjected their own senior ranks, and anyone else they could think of, to an outburst of typically good-humoured wise cracks and sarcastic banter. Then thoughts of rest were put to one side. All else was quickly forgotten as they began to ready themselves and their equipment for the forthcoming action.

Activity levels, along with the atmosphere throughout the crowded corridors of the ship, suddenly changed into a higher gear and became extremely intense. Men rushed backwards and forwards as orders were issued for the necessary ammunition, stores and rations to be drawn. The crew of the *Monarch* were also working flat out as they hurriedly changed from laying tables and preparing meals to getting ready everything on board ship that would be required for the launch of the landing craft. A section of men from one of the troops had stationed themselves in a forward mess deck and were busily filling magazines, checking through personal kit and priming grenades. Suddenly, from somewhere within the small and cramped room, a very loud shout of 'grenade' was heard above the noise level. Someone had accidentally released the safety pin from a primed grenade. An explosion in such a confined and crowded space would have had a devastating and costly effect. But thankfully Lady Luck was smiling. Due to the oppressive heat that had built up inside the room, a hatch above their heads had been left open. Like a game of catch, the grenade was thrown upwards and out through the open hatch where it was caught and tossed overboard to explode harmlessly in the sea. Luckily for all concerned the offending grenade had been primed with a slightly longer fuse than the three-second one that they would use later. This life-threatening incident, like so many others, was quickly forgotten in the hustle of preparations. The outstanding spirit and attitude of the Squadron's men once again showed itself in the eagerness with which they anticipated, and made ready for, their next battle.

Everyone knew that they would be landing from their assault craft in broad daylight. They had also been informed that, since the entire Squadron was on board one vessel, they would have to go ashore in two separate landings. The hastily arranged original plan of attack had been to land them on the western side of the harbour's breakwater but, after new information was received from the Navy, it was decided to land on the eastern side.

The weather had changed totally and was now the complete opposite of what it had been for their first landing. In fact, it was a beautiful balmy sunny summer's evening as *Ulster Monarch* made her approach and started to turn into Augusta harbour. A great bond of trust and friendship had developed between the ship's crew and the men of the Raiding Squadron over the past few months. *Monarch*'s captain, Lieutenant-Commander H.N. Thompson RD RNVR and his crew had actually come to regard the soldiers as something close to brothers in arms, treating them more like some form of royalty than ordinary soldiers; the Squadron, much to everyone's obvious delight, was even included in the naval custom of a daily tot of rum in the morning followed by lime juice in the afternoon.

Music was played constantly over the ship's loudspeaker system for their entertainment and pleasure while quite a few of them, including the officers, indulged in all-day card schools. Gin rummy was the game most favoured by the soldiers; it was played for a penny a point and considerable sums of money changed hands at times. Added to all that obvious enjoyment was the extra bonus of having three hot meals cooked for them each day. With all those things placed alongside their fairly comfortable accommodation they could surely have been forgiven for forgetting about the war and thinking that they were a group of rich tourists on a Mediterranean cruise. But that particular type of relaxed and laid back approach to military life had become the way in which soldiers of the Special Air Service preferred to operate. While 'Who Dares Wins' was to become known as the official motto of the Regiment, an unofficial one for many of its men was 'Train hard, rest easy'. Sid Payne expressed the views held by the majority of his comrades when he made the simple statement: 'When there was no fighting, there was no working.' Lieutenant St John Coates, the ship's paymaster, had obviously been more than suitably impressed by what he had witnessed. In a conversation after the war regarding his time spent in the company of the Squadron he was heard to express the view: 'When those boys hit the beaches you were glad that they were not heading in your direction.'

During their time together Lieutenant Coates also became very aware of the immense pride and very obvious pleasure that Blair Mayne derived from the fact that there were so many brave Irishmen serving and fighting along-side him in the Raiding Squadron. These men, who were all volunteers, came from both sides of the Irish border. He had also expressed his private thoughts to his elder sister Barbara in one of his many letters home: 'I would like to bring this unit home and swagger about Great Britain with them. They look dammed smart; we wear blue shirts with our parachute wings on the left breast.' Their style of dress differed greatly from the norm of the British Army. They wore blue flannel shirts with a black lanyard, khaki drill trousers, brown boots with rubber soles and brown puttees, all topped off with the unique beige-coloured beret and winged dagger badge. Even in the heat of battle very few, if any, of the men ever considered wearing a steel helmet

The attitude of the Squadron towards the crew and officers of *Monarch* was exactly the same. Lance-Corporal Terry Moore even jokingly referred to the ship's captain as 'Captain Cheer'. That title stemmed from his good nature and friendliness towards them, coupled with the fact that they recognised and respected his hard-earned reputation as a skilled and daring naval officer.

The original intention had been for the Squadron to embark into their six landing craft while lying about two miles offshore but, when it was noticed that the defensive boom across the harbour mouth was open, it was felt that this was just too good a chance to be missed. The harbour frontage, the dock area and the white-painted houses with their red-tiled roofs that surrounded the bay were strangely quiet and deceptively peaceful looking. Very shortly it would turn out to be the calm before the storm. Seventeen seaplanes were counted bobbing peacefully up and down on the gentle waves while ships of various shapes and sizes were anchored alongside the docks. As *Monarch* turned and headed straight into the harbour entrance, HMS *Norfolk*, a British cruiser, telegraphed an urgent signal demanding to know just what on earth they thought they were doing. 'I am going in to land my troops' was the very curt reply. After a brief pause the cruiser asked what help they wanted. Once again the answer was short, simple and to the point: 'All that you've got'.

Lieutenant-Commander Thompson's blood was obviously up by that stage and he was certainly in fine fighting form. Perhaps he had a premonition of what was about to happen as he was heard threatening to 'ram this tub onto the beach if needed'. *Ulster Monarch* hove to in the middle of the bay about 300 yards offshore and at 7.30 p.m. began lowering her landing craft. The sections that would be landed in the first wave were loaded quickly and the small boats gunned their engines and headed for the beach. As if this was some form of recognised or prearranged signal for battle to commence, the shore-based enemy guns opened fire. Their heavier shells were exploding all around the larger ships while the landing craft began to attract the brunt of the fire from the heavy machine guns and light anti-aircraft batteries.

The British cruiser and her escort of three destroyers started to return fire. The experienced naval gunners soon found their range and began to bracket the enemy positions. Thousands of tracer rounds glowed brightly as they flashed across the clear blue sky in every direction and hammered relentlessly into their targets. One by one the enemy guns and their crews were blasted into oblivion. The sailors on board one of the smaller naval boats had even decided to get into the action as they steered their craft right up to the edge of the beach to silence an enemy position from pointblank range. Not to be left out of the battle or outdone, the gunners on board *Ulster Monarch*, which by then had steamed back out of the harbour entrance, joined in the barrage with their own small 12-pounder and 20mm cannons. The gun barrels were glowing red hot and steaming as they blazed away as fast as they could be fired and reloaded.

Since there was absolutely nothing that the men of the Raiding Squadron could do, they just crouched down on the bottom of their landing craft. They felt totally helpless as they watched and waited while shell after shell ranged and exploded over and around their heads. A constant and terrifying hail of enemy rounds and shrapnel hammered relentlessly into the armoured fronts and sides of the LCAs. Metal ricocheted wildly off metal before falling into the water where it hissed and made strange patterns all around them. Bob Lowson, a member of No.2 Troop, was standing at the rails of *Monarch* and knew that he would soon have to make a similar journey. Like so many of the others gathered around him all he could do was watch in silence as the small craft carrying his friends suffered under the fierce onslaught.

Many thoughts were running through my mind at that time: how many men would be lost during the landings; would any of our landing craft even survive to make the return trip; and just what could the second wave expect to meet as we tried to make our landing?

At 7.35 p.m. the first landing craft reached the beach and, as the ramps were lowered, the men of No.3 Troop stormed out. Everyone knew that they had to move quickly as they were at their most vulnerable. The twin Vickers machine guns that the men had mounted on the bows opened up immediately. These guns could deliver up to 1,500 rounds per minute of .303 ammunition and were the same weapons that had been used to such great effect on German and Italian airfields in the desert. This was now the Raiders' chance do something about the onslaught of fire to which they had just been subjected and the gunners concentrated mainly on the houses and pillboxes along the sea front where some of the enemy troops had set up their defences.

One of the Squadron's three medical orderlies became the first of two fatalities suffered during the action, sadly not even making it onto the beach alive. He was shot and mortally wounded almost as soon as the landing ramp went down. Even though he was helped out of the water and up onto the beach where he received prompt treatment from the doctor, Phil Gunn, his wounds proved too severe. It would be during the second phase of the landings that the second medic lost his life. He had exited the landing craft just a few short strides in front of Sid Payne when he was struck by a burst of enemy fire. Sid was momentarily stunned because he was only too aware that but for the medic that same burst would almost certainly have killed him. But he knew that he could not stop; there was no real time to think about his own immediate fate, or wonder what might have been.

> Despite the constant fire I bent down and dragged the limp body of the medic out of the water and propped it against a nearby rock. Sadly it really didn't take very long before you got to recognise the signs of death.

All soldiers know only too well that death always poses a threat to them and is a constant companion.

Under the withering covering fire laid down by the Vickers guns, the men of No.3 Troop made their way past the breakwater up the grassy bank and over the sea wall. So far everything had gone according to plan and it had been a fairly good landing. They then began to send men forward into the town itself and at that early stage of the operation no one had any idea of what they would confront. The two medics had been the only men killed during the landings, which, thankfully, had proved much easier than they could either have hoped for or expected. With the main coastal defences having been hammered into silence by the Royal Navy, the primary threat to them was now coming from some sporadic sniper fire. It was strangely quiet and, apart from the sounds of the sniper rounds, there was a ghostly silence hanging over everything. As they began to move closer to the outskirts of the town the brief silence was shattered suddenly by the sound of renewed gunfire.

Lance-Sergeant Andrew Frame was hit and wounded in the neck and shoulder. He had been caught by a burst of heavy machine-gun fire that was being directed at them from a position farther along the coastal road. Frame was suffering badly from severe loss of blood but, despite his injuries, continued to lead his sub-section and stubbornly refused to be sent back to receive treatment. It was obvious to his men that he was in pain but still in charge as he issued orders for them to stop and hold their ground while he moved forward alone to carry out a quick reconnaissance. Information regarding the strength of the enemy on the ground was very limited and so Frame had decided to try and determine the possibility of launching an attack on a nearby pillbox that had just been spotted. Although he was getting weaker by the minute he succeeded in his dangerous task. He had just made his way back and re-assumed command of his section when he received new orders telling them to fall back.

The troop now began the dangerous job of making its way up into and, then, through the town. Their forward movements were being hampered badly by the large amounts of rubble and debris that littered the narrow streets. It was proving very difficult to remain quiet, as they had to edge very slowly and cautiously past the bomb-ravaged and pockmarked buildings. Particular attention had to be paid to every window and door as well as the rooftops for any signs of movement. Cautiously, they dodged from door to door as they covered both sides of the streets and waited for hidden enemy troops to open fire on them. Bursts of heavy gunfire could be heard coming from various parts of the town and, as the sections probed deeper, they began to meet much stiffer resistance. It was slow and highly dangerous work as every single house had to be cleared. Although he was also being extremely careful, Paddy Mayne led his men in his usual way as he strode down the streets in front of them. Hand grenades lobbed into houses, followed by a few long bursts from a machine gun, proved the most effective method of clearing them.

Small scouting patrols were then sent farther forward to try and locate any possible enemy strongpoints or other fortified positions. In particular, they were told to try and locate those that might have been situated in the vicinity of the railway line. That type of information was vital and had to be gathered before any decisions could be taken on any further forward movements. After a brief halt the decision was taken to move again and so they began advancing down towards the railway lines to look for any signs of men from 17 Brigade who were supposed to be waiting for them at a crossroads. The troop split up into its three different sections; one would take the left side, one the right and the third would carry straight on up the main road. They had only made about 200 yds of forward movement when they had a brief engagement with an enemy patrol. The enemy soldiers showed no real stomach for a prolonged action and were easily forced into making a hasty retreat to somewhere close to the outskirts of the town.

Dusk had fallen and nothing else of significance was found in that particular area, so it was decided to play it safe and set up defensive positions. Once these had been established satisfactorily it was felt that another patrol should be sent out to investigate an enemy stronghold that had been spotted near the bridge leading out of town. The patrol was making a cautious approach when the enemy opened up and laid down some very heavy, concentrated fire from

4-inch mortars. They also supported their mortars with an intense barrage of small arms and heavy machine-gun fire. The fire from the MG 34 machine gun was very accurate and appeared to be coming towards them from carefully set up positions. The rounds were ricocheting dangerously in all directions as they glanced off buildings and walls before whining off down the street. It was obvious to the members of the patrol that the enemy were there in fairly substantial numbers. The stronghold was also being given some extra support by armoured vehicles as three light tanks had been spotted manoeuvring and making forward movements.

All three sections from No.3 Troop were coming under increased pressure since they had only their light weapons with which to return fire. They had no support from their mortar team who had been unable to make their way forward. The German troops continued to shell them quite heavily while they constantly tried to probe their positions. One of the light tanks turned its attention towards the troop and began making a menacing move in their direction. One section reacted to the threat and opened fire on the offending tank with a PIAT (Projector, Infantry, Anti-Tank). This cumbersome and unloved weapon was usually fired from the shoulder from a prone position. It weighed about thirty-three pounds and fired a 2¾-pound shell using a spring-loaded mechanism rather than an explosive charge. In reality it was better suited for dealing with soft-skinned or lightly armoured vehicles. The round never really had any chance of destroying the tank or even putting it out of action but the gunner's aim was spot on. Despite the fact that it only glanced harmlessly off the armour plating and buried itself into the roof of a nearby house, the Germans inside had no way of knowing that and were forced to withdraw.

The section holding the ground around the railway station received an unexpected call when the telephone started to ring. It must have been an impulsive reaction but, before he could be stopped, one man picked it up and answered it. The German reaction to the phone call was just as swift and the uneasy quiet that had broken out was shattered about three minutes later by heavy shelling which then continued throughout the rest of the night. Shortly after the shelling had started about twenty or thirty German soldiers were spotted as they began trying to outmanoeuvre one of the other sections. They were probably hoping to use the artillery fire as cover to surprise the men who were holding positions out on the left flank around some petrol storage tanks that were burning fiercely. This move was to prove a fatal error of judgement for them. The section watched them all the way and held their fire as they allowed them to reach a crossroads which was only about fifty yards away. The Germans had made the stupid, but deadly, mistake of bunching too closely together and were just like sitting ducks in a shooting range. Caught in a fierce hail of bullets they had no chance of escape and were cut down in seconds by a mixture of machine-gun and rifle fire. Many were hit and killed outright while the others ran away in complete disarray dropping their weapons and equipment as they went. Sadly the wounded could not be helped and died where they had fallen.

The enemy launched a number of determined and ferocious counter-attacks throughout the night, but each section fought back even harder and returned fire with everything they had. But, as morning approached, the situation for the Raiding Squadron was becoming very precarious. Their radios were out of action, which meant they were unable to call for any form of assistance from the naval gunners, or even report their own positions. The Squadron had also begun to suffer from a very severe shortage of ammunition, a shortage that had been caused by the fact that they had been informed that they were to be involved in a mopping-up operation, 'a piece of cake', as someone had called it earlier. So, because of that information, or lack of it, they had landed with only half their normal supply of ammunition.

The speed with which the operation had been put together and launched was evident in the fact that quite a few men had not even had time to have their meals. Some, including Sid Payne, had just filled their pockets with sausages or whatever they could grab from the dining tables as they passed by and were still trying to eat these when they landed on the beach.

The radio sets that the troops carried with them, No. 11 and No. 19 sets, had been totally drenched by seawater during the landings and were, therefore, useless. Contact with HQ Troop and the other two troops of the Squadron, who were still holding positions in the town centre, was virtually non-existent and so they had been unable to inform them about the substantial increase in the enemy's activities. They also had no way of knowing if Major Mayne was aware of the threat posed by the enemy armour. Uncertainty was added to by the total lack of knowledge of the whereabouts of 17 Brigade with whom they had been supposed to make contact. Understandably, the decision was taken that any further offensive movements were out of the question. There were no clear or valuable targets that could be taken and there was always the possibility of determined German counter-attacks.

Much had changed since the landings and so it had become vital that contact be made between themselves and HQ Troop. Without a moment's hesitation Sergeant John Sillitto, who had been leading one of the forward sections, stepped forward and volunteered to make the return journey. If he was successful he would be able to make a full report about their position and also receive any new orders that needed to be brought back. Faced with a round trip of about a mile, Sillitto wasted no time and set off at once. However, that meagre distance would be a mere stroll in the park for him as he was the man who, rather than face surrender to the Germans, had marched 180 miles out of the desert to return to his unit after an operation. But he still knew that he would have to face some very different and dangerous threats. As well as avoiding the snipers' attention, he would be constantly under very heavy enemy fire. He was an extremely experienced soldier and despite those dangers he managed to return safely with fresh orders. The Troop had been ordered by Mayne to make an immediate withdrawal into the relative safety of the town of Augusta. During the move they again came under heavy enemy fire but, despite that, still managed to make a successful withdrawal without casualties. Defensive positions were immediately thrown up around the outskirts of the town and behind the two bridges leading into it. There was still some intermittent shelling being exchanged by an enemy field gun and the Squadron's mortars, but there were no further major incidents and the night passed off relatively quietly.

During the early hours of 13 July elements of 17 Brigade at long last made contact with the Squadron, relieving them and moving into their former positions to provide cover against any counter-attacks. The Squadron had virtually exhausted its limited supplies of ammunition and there were no guarantees that the enemy was definitely finished. Taking unnecessary chances was something that rarely happened and so it was decided to try to contact any passing naval ships. Two signallers were immediately despatched to the harbour area. Never known to miss an opportunity, the Squadron quickly moved into the town now that they had some hard-earned time to let off steam, relax and enjoy themselves. Bob McDougall could hear the lively sounds of music and singing coming from a nearby building. As he entered he saw one of his old mates, Bill Mitchell, playing what he took to be a piano with great gusto. 'I didn't know you could play an instrument,' he shouted to make himself heard over the noise. He looked around in total amazement at what happened next as the entire place erupted into a large outburst of good-humoured laughter. Strangely, Mitchell never missed a note as he slowly lifted his glass of champagne from the top of the instrument and turned away from it. The music continued because it was, in fact, a type of Pianola that could play itself. As the entertainment progressed the instrument was rolled outside onto the street where Kit Kennedy, complete with top hat, took over the musical duties. A jovial and impromptu party had broken out and the strains of many songs could be heard. 'Lili Marlene', one of the most popular tunes of the day, filled the air. That particular song had crossed the lines from Rommel's soldiers to the men of Eighth Army and had become the anthem of that Army. It had been taken to the hearts of just about every British unit, but most had changed the words to suit themselves. The SAS were no exception and it was Mayne who had written the words that his men were singing. Mayne enjoyed nothing more than having a good old fashioned sing song but, while he was a man who possessed many fine skills, sadly, for those who had to listen, a singing voice was not one of them. In truth he could hardly hold a note.

The vino had started to flow freely and the smells from the many cooking fires filled the air. Some war correspondents, who had been filming the landings, arrived on the scene with their cameras to capture the moment. But they must have been somewhat bemused and rather perplexed by the sights that greeted them. The beige berets had been exchanged for all sorts of non-issue headgear as the men formed up in the town square to pose. One man had even found the essential three-wheeled Italian ice-cream cart and was happily cycling it through the streets.

A few, however, were suffering from the difficult exertions of the last few days and simply took the time to sit quietly and relax in the shade while reflecting on what they had just survived. Others had been detailed to carry out the much more sombre tasks of tending to the wounded or helping to bury their two fallen comrades. Captain Lunt, the Squadron's padre, had asked for some of the wine to be held back for the burial party as he felt that they would need it after their unpleasant duty. He was also very aware that there was a great amount of wine to be consumed as he had personally collected a wheelbarrow filled to overflowing with the finest that could be found. The daily duties of a padre in the field were never done and at times could be very strange. But then the worldly needs of his flock had always to be catered for.

The Pianola proved to be such a favourite with everyone that it was designated by the Squadron for bigger and better things, and so when *Ulster Monarch* made a return visit to Augusta her crew picked it up. (It was certainly put to good use as it stayed with *Monarch* until she was taken out of service many years later.) During the late afternoon a number of small craft were tied together and everyone was ferried across to, and loaded onto, two ships, British and Greek destroyers that had been lying at anchor in Augusta harbour. The soldiers waiting at the dockside were surrounded by a strange array of weapons and suitcases and must have looked like a very motley crew indeed, so much so that the men manning the boats thought that they had been sent in to pick up a bunch of Italian refugees. German bombers suddenly appeared menacingly overhead and immediately launched an air raid. Since the static ships would provide easy targets for the Luftwaffe, they weighed anchor and steamed out to sea at full speed. They made their way to Syracuse harbour where the men of the Squadron were once again transferred back to their mother ship, *Ulster Monarch*.

Earlier the ship's purser had informed a few of the men that he had a simple but very special request. He was an extremely surprised and happy man to find that they had remembered him when he was presented with a much-needed typewriter. That particular item was possibly from the much talked about looting spree that Major Mayne was alleged to have given his men permission to take part in. But there are a few simple facts that should be considered about that incident. Augusta at that time was a town that had just been released from the control of the German army. For the most part, the small Sicilian port was populated by relatively poor people who did not possess any items of outstanding value. It had also suffered greatly and had been virtually destroyed by very heavy bombing and shelling from both sides. Over sixty years ago there were no large shop windows or indeed shops selling expensive gifts, as we know them today. The majority of the so-called loot was cheap commercial goods and large quantities of local wine. The men were only too glad to get their hands on the wine because they were suffering from the cold following the wet landings. The wine that was not consumed was taken back and given to the crew waiting on board their mother ships.

One of the Squadron's cooks, Lance-Corporal 'Clev' Cleverly, much to his obvious delight, had found himself two brand new cooking pots. Typically, like any good cook, he immediately offered to make a fresh brew of tea for everyone. He was somewhat perplexed and annoyed when they declined his generous offer and continued drinking their wine. Although no one ever told him, it might have been due to the fact that there was a strong rumour that the pots had been discovered under a bed. Sid Payne had decided to take a stroll through the streets of the town. As he entered a building he came across the second-in-command of the Squadron, Major Lea, sitting quietly at a table, who said 'Come on in and have a drink of champagne with me'. The Major simply broke the top of the bottle on the edge of the table and handed it to Payne. Incidents like this yet again typified the attitude of all concerned to rank, or lack of it, throughout the Squadron. In another empty building Sid found some pens scattered around in one room and was more than happy to share his finds as he distributed them at random to some passing soldiers. His not so valuable gifts were also accompanied with his express orders: 'Now be sure and write some letters home, lads.'

Two safes had been discovered inside the deserted buildings. On the orders of Major Mayne both were blown open by one of the attached Engineers, but, as with everything else in the small battered town, nothing of any value was discovered. Strange as it may seem, the items most sought after by the majority of men were pieces of lingerie that they knew would be appreciated greatly by wives and girlfriends back home. Perhaps it could also be said that many had the feeling that they had been seen as the expendable part of the greater plan. Some also reckoned that the real lack of any heavy German resistance meant that their commanders had taken the same view as to their fate. The Squadron's daylight landing was to be used as the bait in the trap. They would draw the enemy fire and then the huge British monitor, HMS *Roberts*, that was lying offshore would be presented with easier targets. They surely would also still have been coming to terms with the facts that they had just taken part in and survived what could have been an almost suicidal landing and that Augusta might just have become their final resting place. Or perhaps the simple truth was that they never really gave it much thought. They just regarded it in the way that most soldiers did, and still do.

Major Mayne had an unannounced and very unwelcome visit about looting from a rather pompous captain from the Provost Marshal's office. He was a young officer, full of his own importance, who was certain that he was going to get to the bottom of the incident and arrived looking like some sort of avenging angel. However, things did not go according to his plan. It turned out to be a short sharp meeting indeed and the hapless officer found himself being given a huge helping hand as he made his somewhat unceremonious and ungainly exit through the door. He left the building more quickly than he had entered and, although he did not know it, could count himself extremely lucky. When confronted by that type of person, Blair Mayne usually made a point of choosing the nearest window for the exit of his unwanted visitor. He was also never known to check if the chosen window was open at that time. That brief encounter was certainly not his first run in with the Redcaps and nor would it be his last. Mayne never tried to hide the fact that he viewed people who conducted themselves in that manner with the utmost contempt. Yes, he most certainly understood that they had a necessary job to do but they did not have to enjoy doing it quite so much.

The landing and subsequent actions at Augusta cost the Special Raiding Squadron the lives of two of its medical orderlies, Corporal John Bentley and Private George Shaw, while a further eight soldiers were wounded. The Squadron had been very lucky as the price paid could have been much higher. These men had just taken part in the capture of the first major enemy harbour in Europe and this had been achieved in a daylight raid. If they had met with the expected stiff resistance it could easily have been turned into another tragedy like Dieppe. As a direct consequence of the successful operation the German forces had suffered considerable alarm and the loss of much valuable equipment. A German spokesman at that time described it as 'A night of terror the Germans will never forget'. A later report from a German newspaper stated:

> We had suffered absolute hell from the Royal Air Force bombing and from the accuracy of the naval shelling, but it was the last straw when in daylight a British Parachute Regiment (the Raiding Squadron) landed at Augusta. We were helpless, machine guns, artillery and mortars were turned on them but they still came on, nothing could stop them.

A quite unexpected bonus from the landing was the discovery and capture of a German submarine. Her crew must have found it impossible to make their escape and had submerged in the harbour.

An Army newspaper was circulated to the troops in which one of the main features was an article about the men of the Special Raiding Squadron. Contained in the paper was an article written by an army commander that drew particular attention to their conduct both in and out of action. He also made a reference to their considerably high standards of discipline, dress and fitness.

The landing at and capture of Augusta turned out to be the last action undertaken by the Special Raiding Squadron in Sicily. For their parts in the operation, two men were decorated: Lance-Sergeant Frame was awarded the Military Medal and Sergeant Sillitto was awarded a Bar to his Military Medal.

Operations on Sicily had been expected to last about ninety days but were so successful that they lasted for only thirty-eight. Approximately 200,000 Axis prisoners were taken while the number of Germans killed or wounded totalled not less than 23,000. Italian losses were not as severe and were in the region of 7,000 to 8,000 casualties. Between 1 July and 17 August Axis aircraft losses totalled 1,691. Allied forces lost approximately 19,000 men either wounded or killed and 274 aircraft.

Chapter VIII

Bagnara: A Foothold on the Italian Mainland

Following resupply with stores and ammunition from the newly established depots at Syracuse, the Squadron re-embarked on their landing craft during the morning of 15 July. However, they were not heading into action but being taken back to Capo-Murro-di-Porco to review the scene of their initial success. The soldiers needed no prompting to make the best of their brief interlude by using the time to rest and relax, enjoying themselves as they swam and played about in the warm blue waters of the Mediterranean like a bunch of children on a Sunday school outing. There was a strange, but understandable, sense of sadness hanging over some, as they imagined how, not so very long ago, those same innocent looking waters had claimed the lives of so many unfortunate and brave airborne soldiers. For a brief time they had been given the chance to share in a rare sense of freedom; stories and memories were exchanged as well as the usual cheerful banter. A few took time to retrace their steps and reminisce about their very recent actions. But the strangely calm and peaceful conditions fooled no one; everyone knew that this would be only a short-lived respite since, at a moment's notice, they could be called back into action again.

It was also on such days that Paddy Mayne would have taken the chance to relax with his men and enjoy himself. He would almost certainly have been feeling tremendous pride in the fact that his small unit had once again not only justified their existence but also proved that it was more than capable of accomplishing any tasks that might be required of it in the near future. Every soldier under his command knew without any doubt that Mayne was a fair and approachable officer who would listen to any of their suggestions, worries or ideas. Even though he was still only 28 years old, he was perhaps ten years older than most of them and, therefore, regarded by them as the elder statesman of the regiment. They valued his opinion and trusted his judgement without question. One junior officer even spoke of him as being 'more like a university tutor than a commanding officer'. That was almost certainly due to the way in which he would try to help resolve their concerns and discuss their various problems, military or otherwise. Mayne seemed to have the ability to sense when difficulties occurred amongst his soldiers, to whom he was an outstanding and charismatic leader, inspiring not only great courage but also absolute dedication. His men were prepared to lay down their lives for him. It was possibly because he knew this that he was always very wary of some of the plans and schemes drawn up for them by senior officers.

Mayne had a huge presence and in battle or a tight spot those around him felt that he was invincible and indestructible. To his soldiers he was the consummate warrior and the ultimate in fighting men. Terry Moore, who had fought alongside Mayne throughout the desert campaigns and knew him extremely well, said of him: 'When in battle he was like a machine, but a machine with a brain, and in his own mind's eye he had it spot on.' Moore personally witnessed an event that occurred in Sicily that certainly seemed to lend credence to the ever-growing legend surrounding Mayne.

> During a brief lull in the action Paddy had decided to stop with a few of us and take a quick break for a dixie of tea. Tony Marsh, Darkie Jones, Chalky White, Kit Kennedy, Bob Lilley and I were standing beside him when we suddenly heard the familiar whistling sound of an incoming mortar round. We were left with absolutely no time to move before the 4-inch shell landed smack in the middle of our small group. To be more precise it landed right between the slightly splayed feet of Paddy Mayne. It somehow remained balanced upright for a few seconds before it finally spluttered and harmlessly fell over. Luckily for us it must have been a dud and just didn't explode. Some people may say that it was the luck of the Irish that saved us while others will maintain that you make your own in circumstances like that.

As with so many others over the previous few years that incident was taken in their stride. What they had witnessed might have turned others into nervous wrecks but Paddy Mayne and his men were made of much sterner stuff and carried on as if nothing had happened. During an earlier conversation between the two men, David Stirling had described the Special Air Service as being like 'pawns on a large chessboard'. That was a simple analogy that Paddy Mayne understood and agreed with wholeheartedly. But there was much more to Mayne than being an officer and a fighting soldier. He was a young man with an extremely good education who was well read in many subjects; but he also had a philosophical outlook on life. On more than one occasion he had been overheard saying, either to himself while in deep thought or when speaking to his men: 'There you are, you see what have I always said: history is simply repeating itself.' There was only a short interlude before the Squadron was recalled and ferried back to its waiting mother ship. *Ulster Monarch* made her way back to Augusta and, as she entered the harbour, sailed slowly past two commando ships, HMS *Queen Emma* and HMS *Prinses Beatrix*, which were lying at anchor. Shortly after his return Major Mayne was summoned to attend a conference on board *Beatrix*. It had been called to discuss plans for a landing at Catania. Those at the conference included the commanding officers of Nos 3 Army and 40 (Royal Marine) Commandos as well as three staff officers representing General Montgomery. The proposed plan called for No.3 Commando to be landed north of Catania to set up and hold a temporary bridgehead. Once that objective had been achieved the Raiding Squadron would then be landed as the spearhead of the operation to fight its way inland to capture and hold the dock area.

The suggested landing area meant that they would be expected to cover a distance of five miles before they even approached the docks. The third part of the plan called for No.40 (RM) Commando to follow up behind the Squadron to form an outer defensive ring around the captured docks. Everyone at the conference agreed that it was a great plan in theory, but most were left in little doubt that it would turn out to be yet another form of slaughter, but on a much grander and very costly scale. Thankfully for all concerned the attack was called off at the last moment when news came through that the German commanders had rushed up more troops to reinforce the proposed landing areas.

During the night the *Luftwaffe* raided Augusta port and the harbour area was filled with the ear-splitting sounds of the constant barrage from heavy anti-aircraft guns and the chatter of the light AA weapons. Added to that cacophony were the screams from diving bombers and the whine and thud of exploding bombs as the enemy pilots searched out and, in some cases, found their targets. *Queen Emma* fared very badly during the raid and suffered several heavy hits; sixty-three men from the commando units billeted on board her sustained wounds and sixteen were killed. An order for the Squadron to disembark from *Ulster Monarch* was issued hastily as she was being sent back out to sea where she could hopefully find relative safety. Once the Squadron had been put ashore its members immediately began the job of setting up a new camp around the port.

At first light next morning it was business as usual as they continued with yet more general training. Later in the day they boarded new types of vessels, American landing craft infantry (LCIs), and took part in a practice landing. These were much larger vessels than *Ulster Monarch*, at nearly 160 feet in length, and could carry 188 men. Each craft had a top speed of 16 knots and was manned by a crew of twenty-four. They had been specifically designed and built for the task of landing assault troops with all their equipment and many of them had been supplied to the Royal Navy.

Major Mayne called a briefing to inform his men that orders had just been issued for them to land at Capo-D'Ali and demolish the road and railway lines there. However, due to the speed at which Eighth Army was moving forward, the operation was cancelled at the last minute. Such cancellations were commonplace for special forces but still caused great annoyance for everyone and revived memories of the early days of inactivity and frustration in the Commando units.

Some good news did reach them the following morning when they were informed that men from the Durham Light Infantry, who formed part of Montgomery's Eighth Army, had won their battle and recaptured the Primosole Bridge. The pace of events now meant that the Squadron's talents would be required elsewhere and so, once again, it was on the move, this time by yet another form of transport as the men boarded the carriages of a train. Their next destination was to be Cannizzaro, just north of Catania, where they set up yet another temporary camp. Normal day-to-day life continued and, as ever, high standards were demanded; there was never any reason for standards to be allowed to fall in the SAS. Any lack of discipline was dealt with swiftly and seven men who had abandoned their positions without orders, and for no good reason, during the heavy fighting at Augusta were returned to their parent units.

Over the next few weeks the Squadron continued its usual tough regime of exercise and general training. At times living conditions were very harsh and difficult for everyone, but overall they had started to show some signs of improvement and there were, of course, many lighter moments to relieve the monotony of camp life. Their diet in the field was based on the standard rations of the Army, bully beef and hard biscuits. The latter could be adapted for several purposes including porridge, for which it had first to be hammered, or even pudding. A good cook could work wonders even with such basic ingredients and a little time but the Squadron did not have cordon bleu standard chefs. However, the monotony of bully beef and biscuit was broken by the availability of other ration foods, including a meat and vegetable stew, tinned fish (usually intended as a breakfast dish), bacon rashers, the unpleasant looking but palatable soya links, some cheese and even marmalade. Some soldiers ate their breakfast biscuits with cheese and marmalade to soften the baked item. Bread was rare and available only when near a field bakery.

By this stage in the war, much attention had been given to the problem of feeding soldiers in the field and new ration packs had been devised and were being issued. These were the Compo (for composite) packs that provided more variety and were issued to offer a more varied menu over a few days for a small group, such as the crew of a tank, or for one day for a platoon of infantry. Of course, there was always plenty of local, if strange, food-stuff, such as olives, tomatoes and almonds but, given half a chance, soldiers would supplement the basics with

Italian operations, showing Bagnara

whatever could be bought or scrounged from the locals or 'found' on their travels.

One such occasion occurred when one of the Squadron snipers used his skills with a rifle and procured a sheep for the communal cooking pot. Dougie Monteith found himself being enlisted to assist with the preparation of the animal. In a very short time he had the animal skinned, gutted and ready for the pot. But as Dougie was working on the carcass he became aware that a rather interested local was keeping an extremely close watch on his every move.

> I could feel his beady eyes burning into the back of my neck and every time I looked over my shoulder the old boy was just standing there, just staring at me. A few sharp and carefully chosen words, plus some internationally recognised hand gestures, sent the man disappearing swiftly into the distance. But every time I glanced backwards the same old man was again standing right behind me.

It later transpired that he was a shepherd and the owner of the unfortunate animal. After a brief discussion he finally agreed to leave the camp when he was told that he could have the head, fleece and feet of the sheep to take home with him. 'God only knows why he wanted those bits but who were we to argue when we had taken what we wanted.'

Long periods without action could cause problems for everyone and have a severe effect on morale. Paddy Mayne always tried to find things to occupy his troops and ensure that they never had any dull moments. At his

express orders the entire Squadron, including the very
irate cooks, had to take it in turns to make the physically
demanding and exhausting climb up to the summit of
the nearby volcano. That it happened to be Mount Etna,
which was nearly 11,000 feet and one of the most active
and highly dangerous in the world, never even raised an
eyebrow. In Mayne's mind it just added another factor to
the excitement of the day. The only men allowed to miss
the hazardous climb were the sick and wounded but they
had to be officially excused duties by the Medical Officer,
Captain Phil Gunn. One of the happy soldiers was Sid
Payne and it was probably the only time that he felt good
about the fact that an old leg wound he had received in the
desert had been playing him up. Having made the exhausting and dangerous climb some of the men decided to hold
an impromptu celebration at the top of the volcano. Their
Commanding Officer was, as usual, right in the thick of
festivities, but things were not going to his liking. 'There
is too much talking going on here and not enough drinking, from now on we'll have ten minutes' drinking time
and then ten minutes' talking time.' All went well until
Captain Tony Marsh got his timings wrong and spoke out
of turn. A well aimed right hook from Mayne stopped
him in mid sentence and laid him out cold. Nobody even
blinked at what had just happened. Marsh had simply
broken the rules that had been laid down.

Captain Lunt, the padre, had also been very busy looking
after the spiritual needs of his flock by conducting open-air
church services. Those events took place despite an obvious lack of desire by the soldiers to take part. During one
service the padre was so deep in thought and concentration
as he led the singing of a hymn that he failed to hear the

ominous drone of an approaching German Messerschmitt Bf109 fighter. It was only when he looked up from his open prayer book and saw that he was standing completely on his own while everyone else was running hell for leather to find cover that the penny finally dropped. He lost no time in joining his swiftly disappearing choir as they headed for the nearest shelter.

On 1 September the Squadron was ordered to move once more, this time to Catania where yet another new camp was established close to the beach. Ironically, this was the very beach that, only a few weeks earlier, might have become the final resting place for many of the Squadron's men. The Officers' Mess had been set up in an upstairs room of a two-storey building while everyone else was billeted in tents in the surrounding courtyard. They were extremely well practised in setting up camp by now and had quickly slipped into the familiar routine of cooking, cleaning and general maintenance. Of course, all those worthwhile jobs were carried out alongside partaking of the occasional bottle of local wine.

One evening the men found themselves coming under very accurate aerial attack. However, it was not enemy fire being directed at them but Paddy Mayne who, in rather jovial mood after consuming a few bottles of the local produce, had decided to indulge in some impromptu target practice. His aim, as always, was good and he showered anyone who could be seen below with a large selection of flowerpots taken from a window of the mess. That short bombardment was a very mild and placid outburst from him. His men were well used to his fun and games; a few had been bodily thrown into and out of jeeps or trucks, while others had been driven over by them. They had also been shot at, dragged from their tents, usually to accompany him on some wild scheme or drinking spree, or chased from camp and out into the wilds of the desert. Some had even been lifted by one of his huge hands and thrown out of the nearest window. It must be said that, on many occasions, he found himself accompanied by more than a few willing participants in his pranks. However, drinking was only ever allowed when not in action; this was one rule that was adhered to strictly.

Living on their wits and off the land for so long had taught them that everything had more than one use. Many less well-educated people who visited their camps were horrified to see that they even made their tents secure by tying them down with rolls of cordite fuse. David Danger nearly found himself in deep trouble when he allowed an engineer to talk him into helping with a prank. A small piece of the fuse was to be lit and used as an improvised firecracker and it was to be Danger who would have the honour of throwing it. Danger was a good soldier and an excellent signaller but had no real idea of how powerful an explosion this device might cause.

It exploded with a rather sharp bang and threw up a shower of small stones that grazed slightly the leg of a watching bystander. Thankfully for me, the incident caused a bit of a stir for a few moments but was then simply put down as being high spirits among us and it was never mentioned again.

New orders were received and the raiders began making preparations for their next task which was to be yet another amphibious landing under the code name of

Operation BAYTOWN, in which the Squadron's objectives were to capture, occupy and hold Bagnara Calabria, a small town on Italy's west coast. If the landings were successful the Squadron was then to advance and prevent the enemy from destroying any of the important bridges or installations that could delay the main forces, which were to follow up. The landings and subsequent actions to be carried out by the Squadron were only a small part of the overall Allied plans for the invasion of Italy. But they were of vital importance and needed to be carried out successfully. Eighth Army, under Montgomery, was to cross the Straits of Messina for the landings at Reggio and then drive through Calabria to join up with the United States Fifth Army under General Mark Clark, which was to land at Salerno in Operation AVALANCHE on 9 September. There was also to be a subsidiary landing by the British 1st Airborne Division with the task of capturing the Italian naval base at Taranto; this was Operation SLAPSTICK.

Bagnara was a small coastal town accessible by only one small road that twisted tortuously up through the cliffs and into the hills leading to the surrounding plateau. The narrow road wound its way across bridges and through tunnels hewn from the cliff faces.

At 2.00 p.m. on 1 September the men of the SRS boarded LCIs 179 and 274 at Catania and made their way to Riposto. After an uneventful passage they arrived at 6.00 p.m. and spent the rest of the night making their preparations. Throughout the following two days various problems occurred with their two craft; 179 fouled a propellor that had to be freed by one of the Squadron while the other one ran aground. But finally, at 8.00 p.m.

on 3 September, the Squadron set sail in LCI 179 along with five LCAs. At 4.45 a.m. the majority of the men had disembarked and made a safe landing on the northern beach of Bagnara Calabria from four of the LCAs. After a brief, but very sharp, discussion it was discovered that the landing on that particular stretch of beach was due to an error in navigation on the part of the naval officers, an error that meant they were roughly one mile out in their calculations. The initial intention had been to land the Squadron farther to the south but it later transpired that this had been a fortunate error indeed. The northern beach had been sown very heavily with mines and was also booby-trapped. But there was a negative side to the mistake; the delays to the landings had been very costly and meant that the plan was now running dangerously behind schedule. They had also lost the much-desired cover of darkness as dawn was beginning to break. It had been a deathly quiet morning and, strangely, the Squadron had met no opposition as the first few men started landing.

By 5.15 a.m. the last men had disembarked and all thoughts were beginning to turn to the job at hand. Suddenly, from somewhere farther inland, they heard the sound of some large explosions. The general consensus was that they were too late after all and that the blasts were demolition charges being detonated. The men of Nos 3 and 2 Troops immediately began spreading out to set up defensive positions around the beach area and the outskirts of Bagnara. The town turned out to be virtually deserted with most houses and buildings empty. But the caves and tunnels in the hillside surrounding it were packed to over-flowing with hundreds of very frightened Italian civilians.

They had obviously fled in fear when the explosions started but when they made the discovery that the newly-arrived troops were British they poured out to welcome them and celebrate their totally unexpected liberation from their German oppressors. 'Inglesi, Inglesi', they screamed and cheered as the totally bewildered soldiers looked on and watched the approaching masses. The vast majority of the inhabitants were, after all, just poor peasants who had been caught up in a war that was not of their making. Just as in Augusta many houses were plastered with graffiti in support of Mussolini; 'Viva Il Duce' covered the walls. But the local inhabitants certainly gave the impression that they had no love for Mussolini's Fascists or their German allies.

A Section, No.1 Troop had just begun their advance into the heart of the town when they spotted a company of German troops marching round a bend on the main road about forty yards behind them. Strangely, or stupidly, the Germans seemed to be totally unaware that any landings had taken place; they were marching along with their rifles and other weapons slung over their shoulders. Despite being taken aback by the Germans' sudden appearance behind them, the Section's Bren gunner opened fire. His quick reactions to the surprise situation meant that five German soldiers were hit and wounded while another twenty-eight were rounded up and taken prisoner. Among the various items of equipment recovered from them were three MG 34 machine guns. At 900 rounds per minute the firepower of those weapons was devastating and they also made a very distinctive noise that sounded like paper being ripped. Everyone was glad that at least they would not have to face those particular MG 34s. That brief and successful skirmish was to be the first engagement in what would

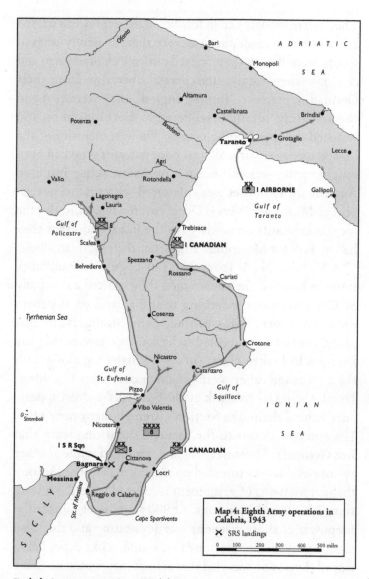

Eighth Army operations in Calabria

turn out to be a very long and hard day for the members of the Raiding Squadron.

The men of B and C Sections of No.1 Troop were not to be so fortunate on their move forward, however, as they were met with a deadly onslaught of heavy machine-gun and mortar fire. Two soldiers from the sections were caught by the fierce fire and killed outright while seven others received serious wounds. Some men, having seen what had just happened, tried to move up and rescue their comrades from what was turning into a very serious situation. The dead and wounded were lying in the middle of the road where they had fallen and the enemy machine gunners continued to pour fire into them. The Germans realised instantly what the others were trying to do when they spotted their movements and laid down an even heavier barrage onto the road. Brave and undoubtedly committed as they were, the ferocity and accuracy of the enemy fire forced them to retreat. One man, Private Richard Higham, however, felt that he had spotted a solution to the problem when he noticed a small gutter that ran alongside the road. He knew instinctively that there was no time to waste and so decided not to wait for any help. Acting alone, he took his chance and by using the gutter as cover was able to crawl up alongside the casualties. Private Higham showed total disregard for the continuous enemy fire thrown at him and managed to bring the wounded and dead back one by one. Although he had been successful in bringing them out of the direct line of fire, the wounded were still in grave danger from enemy mortars.

Phil Gunn, the Squadron's Medical Officer, had been watching these events unfold and waiting for his chance to step in and help. He saw the opening that he had been hoping for and moved forward immediately to begin treating the wounded men. Captain Gunn was certainly one of the Squadron's busiest men and on many occasions he could have been regarded as one of their bravest since, most of the time, he had to treat casualties in the open under enemy fire.

B Section was still continuing its advance while C Section remained in the town to hold the defensive positions. Seemingly oblivious to the heavy fire being directed at them, Lance-Sergeant William McNinch was leading his sub-section cautiously down the road that led directly out of the town. Moving slowly and surely they were able to keep making progress and eventually got to within 200 yards of the enemy positions. There was little or no cover and the ground over which they were moving was rock-hard and barren. But, undeterred, the small group kept pushing forward until at last they were able to find some worthwhile protection. From his new position Lance-Sergeant McNinch was able not only to control and direct his own men's fire towards the Germans but also act as a spotter for some of the other sections' guns. Suddenly, from somewhere up on the higher terraced ground above them, the Germans brought another Spandau machine gun into action.

Now the raiders were in an extremely dangerous situation as they found themselves coming under an almost incredible fusillade of fire. The sub-section's Bren gunner was Private John Tunstall and he was returning the enemy fire with added interest but, unknown to him, his position was being given away by the tell-tale flash of the tracer rounds that he had loaded into his magazines. The

German gunners were able to locate him quite easily by following the flight of the tracers and began to home in on him. It must have seemed to Tunstall as if he had just become the prime target for every gunner in the area as he started to come under a fierce torrent of fire. Before very long the German gunners found their mark and Tunstall was raked by a heavy and accurate burst of fire. Luckily for him, the Bren took the main force of the rounds and was blasted out of his hands. But a round finally found its mark and passed right through his cheeks. He sustained further wounds to his face from shrapnel, and splinters from the stock of his weapon. The sheer force of the rounds hammering into the Bren had been so great that he was knocked over and sent tumbling backwards. Although visibly shaken by what had just happened, Tunstall was not wounded too badly and was able to crawl back to his original position. Lance-Sergeant McNinch quickly took control of the situation and dressed his injuries before getting him back into action. Despite the fact that at one stage he and his men had been completely cut off and surrounded, McNinch still carried on returning fire and also relayed much needed information about enemy movements to the other sections.

No.2 Troop had also made the move from the beach shortly after the other sections and had begun making its southward move cautiously on a route planned to take the Troop up through the town and out onto the main road. The soldiers had covered only a relatively short distance when the leading section came across a bridge that seemed to have been demolished recently. It was agreed that the damage had very probably been caused by the explosions that had been heard earlier. Captain Tony Marsh immediately ordered the men of his section to halt and take up defensive positions while another section was ordered to push farther up the road. Lieutenant Peter Davis was leading the latter Section which he split into two smaller groups before trying to make progress up into the terraced hills surrounding the town.

However, the Germans dug in above them had been watching intently and quickly spotted their moves. They opened up and started to hammer Davis's men with heavy concentrated fire. Private Charlie Tobin died almost instantly when he was caught in the open and hit by the full force of a prolonged machine-gun burst. The force of the rounds hitting him was so great that they very nearly cut him in two. Looking back down into the town one of the sections spotted a German patrol trying to move out of their positions close to a clock tower. A few heavy bursts of fire were loosed off in their direction. Those Germans who were not killed by the initial volleys were soon mopped up and taken prisoner by another section. Yet more German troops were dug in and holding positions above the Squadron in the steep hills around Bagnara and they had started to lay down heavy and accurate mortar fire. Major Mayne wanted some first-hand intelligence and so he had also been on the move. After leaving his command post in the town centre, he had made his way quickly past the blown bridge and was just ahead of No.2 Troop. He had stopped at a bend in the road where he was studying some aerial photographs and directing operations. Paddy Mayne knew that the situation was extremely dangerous and changing rapidly so he held a conference with Captain Harry Poat and, after a short exchange of views, issued him with new orders for troop movements and positions.

Lance-Corporal James McDiarmid had command of a sub-section and was leading his men in an easterly direction out of the town when they also came under very heavy fire. McDiarmid was hit by a volley of fire and wounded in the ankle, but his first thoughts were for the safety of the men in his charge. Immediately he decided to send his men back without him. Although in pain he totally disregarded his wounds and remained where he had fallen; his intention was to provide the others with enough covering fire for their safe withdrawal. Once he saw that his men had reached relative safety he crawled back to rejoin them. Despite a severe loss of blood he chose to move again and started to lead his section back into the hills. McDiarmid hoped to try and outflank the enemy gun positions that were causing all the problems and silence them for good.

Pushing on farther forward the men of B Section again started to come under sustained machine-gun and rifle fire. This heavy fire forced them to take cover and made it virtually impossible for them to make any more progress until darkness fell. However, C Section were slightly luckier as they continued to move on uphill where they took up some new positions. No.3 Troop had also moved on and was making its way through the town towards the southern outskirts. The Germans were watching everything very intently and the Troop was spotted making its move. Enemy gunners opened up with their 4-inch mortars supported by a variety of small arms fire. Fearing that they could become pinned down under the onslaught, No.3 Troop launched an immediate attack and after a short and fierce firefight the Germans were forced to leave their positions and retreat. The fleeing German soldiers abandoned their mortars and took cover in a nearby tunnel. But they did not stay in the tunnel for very long, perhaps realising that they had just run into a dead end. Those who could simply took to their heels and ran away. They left behind ten dead along with three wounded and many more who would become prisoners.

At 11.00 a.m. and then again at 2.00 p.m. the mortars which had been set up in the town along with Headquarter Troop opened fire. The first few rounds were to test out the strength of the enemy positions and, secondly, to combat the serious threat posed by the enemy sniper and machine-gun fire. The fire was, as usual, very accurate and found its targets with rounds landing on both the road and bridge. This had the desired effect as all the enemy fire was silenced and the remainder of the night passed fairly quietly. As dawn broke on the morning of 5 September the Mortar Platoon was again in action, ranging in on the same targets as the previous day; once again they were successful. Many more of the offending enemy sniper and machine-gun positions were silenced.

Throughout the various actions around Bagnara the Mortar Platoon's members were always in the thick of the fighting and fired over 300 rounds in support and defence of the troops on the ground. During one particularly heavy engagement, Private George Bass, a loader in one of the three-man teams, was hurling rounds into the mouth of the mortar tube as fast as they were passed to him. Round in ... wumph ... round in ... wumph ... round in ... nothing ... round in ... nothing ... silence. George knew immediately what he had just done. Two live rounds had been dropped down the tube at the same time. The other two members of the team looked at each other in disbelief for a few seconds and then turned to stare at George. They did not jump about or panic in any way but said simply: 'Well George, it's like this, you put them in there so you can get them out all by yourself.' George found himself faced with the unenviable task of having to upend the mortar tube and empty the two live rounds out onto the ground. He knew that he had no other choice. Once he had the rounds in front of him he picked them up and placed one under each arm before moving out to find the nearest empty ditch in which to dispose of them. Incidents such as this were not a common occurrence in the Squadron but everyone knew that mistakes did happen and when they did would almost always have to be rectified while under heavy enemy fire. Even while operating under such dangerous conditions the team still somehow managed to see a funny side, although it must be said that George Bass did not find that particular incident quite so funny as his two comrades until much later.

B Section of No.1 Troop spotted an Italian patrol as it was making its way down the main road towards them. Despite the fact that the Italians were about 600 yards away they decided to open fire on them. Even at that extreme distance their fire proved very accurate and they watched as two of the patrol were hit and killed. The other Italians wasted no time in scattering very quickly in all directions. Orders had just started coming through telling the Squadron to leave their positions and make their way to Favazzina. In the meantime a patrol by C Section, No.2 Troop under Derrick Harrison had been sent out to the western ridge to try to locate a German 88mm gun battery that had been shelling the town heavily and causing many problems. The patrol, of six men, set off and carefully made its way forward and up into the terraced hills.

No enemy patrols were sighted or encountered and so they continued making good progress through some heavily wooded areas. After making initial radio contact with headquarters, which had been successful, all further contact was lost. Inadequate, faulty or just useless equipment was a huge factor that continued to plague the signallers throughout the Sicilian and Italian campaigns. Their radios were not good enough to do the job that they had been expected to do. From the height advantage afforded to them by the hills, the patrol spotted a small village and began cautiously making their way down into it. They need not have been worried about their safety because the villagers of Regna-del-Fiuma welcomed them with open arms and informed them that the Germans had already left the area.

Outside the village they made contact with forward elements of 1st Green Howards, from 15 Infantry Brigade (this was a Regular Army brigade of 5th Division and included three regular Yorkshire battalions: 1st Green Howards; 1st King's Own Yorkshire Light Infantry and 1st York and Lancaster Regiment. The brigade commander at this time was Brigadier E.O. Martin). They also encountered a Brigadier who was having a rest and eating lunch at his HQ. He gave the impression of being quite happy and at ease with the world and also seemed unconcerned and oblivious to the events that had been taking place all around him. The enemy gun position was eventually located in the hills overlooking the small village of Pellegrina. It was surrounded by a large number of spent shell cases but was totally deserted and abandoned. As the patrol made its way down into the village two Italian soldiers decided that they had done enough for the cause and presented themselves for capture. A further two, however, had obviously been feeling somewhat braver than their countrymen and opened fire from their concealed position in the hillside. It did not take very long for Harrison and his men to find the position and the pair was also taken prisoner. At 4.00 p.m. on 5 September Lieutenant Derrick Harrison and his patrol returned safely and handed over their four captives along with some captured documents to Divisional HQ in Bagnara where they spent the night.

The overall strength of the enemy forces on the ground was hard to determine throughout the operation at Bagnara but some captured German soldiers asked questions about their comrades from other battalions. The Germans who had been killed or captured belonged either to Jäger, Grenadier or Sapper Regiments. In general terms, German troops on the ground were of fairly good quality and also very experienced; some were veterans from the African and Russian fronts.

A brief résumé of the operation broke the Squadron's casualties down to: 50 percent from very accurate mortar fire; 30 percent from machine-gun fire; and 20 percent from sniping. The Bagnara operation had resulted in five men being killed in action: Signalman C Richards, Signalman W. Howell, Signalman Parris and Private C. Tobin, all of whom died on 4 September. Private Ball died on 5 September from wounds received on the 4th.

Seventeen men were wounded: Sergeant Badger, Lance-Sergeant Shaw, Corporal Mitchell, Lance-Corporals McDiarmid, Little, Thurston and Wortly, Signalmen Midgely and Hill, Privates Bryson, Clarke, Glacken,

Grimster, Kirk, Squires, Tunstall and Wilson. Tunstall's wounds were so severe that after twelve months of medical care he was deemed unfit for any further military service.

Captain Phil Gunn was awarded the Military Cross while Lance-Sergeant McNinch, Lance-Corporal McDiarmid, and Privates Higham and Tunstall were awarded the Military Medal.

The enemy sustained eighty-two casualties of all ranks

At 3.00 p.m. on 5 September the Special Raiding Squadron embarked for Messina in Sicily for rest and re-organisation.

1. A young Blair Mayne at home during his university days. (Menown)

2. An early photograph of Mayne in uniform. The black buttons suggest that the photograph was taken after his transfer from the Royal Artillery to the Royal Ulster Rifles. (BMAssn)

3. Above; As a young subaltern at the SAS base at Kabrit. Note the new wings. (John Martin)

4. Right: David Danger. Known as a great signaller, he served from the early days at Kabrit. (Danger)

5. Alex Skinner MM. Killed in the lorry explosion at Termoli. (Bass)

6. Taffy Leadbetter. Also killed at Termoli. (Bass)

7. Jack Nixon. This photograph was taken on his wedding day in 1944 when he was only 19 years old. (Nixon)

8. Alex Muirhead. Taken during training for the invasion of Sicily. After the war he became chief medical officer for the BBC. (Muirhead)

9. Alex Muirhead at Termoli. In his own words he was 'not praying, just watching a German Bf109 flying overhead'.

10. Douglas Monteith. (Monteith)

1. Bob McDougall. (McDougall)

12. Terry Moore MM. (Brossier)

13. Joe Fassam.

14. Sid Payne. (Payne)

15. Bob Lowson. Photographed during his time with the Middle East Commando. (Lowson)

16. The Winged Dagger badge of the SAS. (Author's collection)

17. Terry Moore and Frank Jocelyn. (Brossier)

MOTOR VESSEL "ULSTER MONARCH." 3,800 TONS.
LIVERPOOL-BELFAST EXPRESS SERVICE.
ULSTER IMPERIAL LINE (BELFAST STEAMSHIP CO LTD)

18. HMS *Ulster Monarch*.

19. Some members of the newly formed Mortar Troop, early 1943.

20. Landing Craft Infantry or LCI. (BMAssn)

21. An LCA alongside HMS *Ulster Monarch*. (McDougall)

2. Training hard – rock and cliff scaling. (McDougall)

23. On leave in Tel Aviv. L-R: Paddy Kenna, Ginger Hodgkinson, Bob McDougall, Darkey Rogerson and Ginger Hines. (McDougall)

24. General Sir Bernard Montgomery making a speech to the SRS on board HMS *Ulster Monarch*. (McDougall)

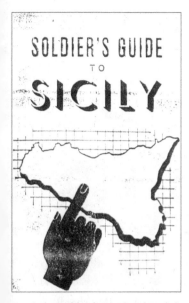

25. 'The Soldier's Guide to Sicily', a booklet issued to all soldiers aboard the invasion fleet. (Author's collection)

26. Captured enemy anti-aircraft gun being pressed into British service. (Muirhead)

7. Captured, the second gun battery. (Muirhead)

28. Captured coastal defence guns at Capo Murro-di-Porco. (Muirhead)

29. A short rest after the final battle for the guns. (Muirhead)

30. Sorting out kit at Syracuse with 'Buttercup' Joe Goldsmith in the foreground. (Sid Payne)

31. Augusta Harbour postcard. (Danger)

32. A street in Augusta. (Danger)

33. Termoli railway station. (Sid Payne)

34. Members of C Section, No. 2 Troop. On the right with his hand in his pocket is Alex Gilmore. He lost an eye at Termoli. (Sid Payne)

35. Officers and men of No. 2 Troop. (Sid Payne)

36. A devastated street after an explosion outside a monastery in Termoli. (Sid Payne)

37. Aerial reconnaissance photograph of Bagnara. (George Bass)

38. The grave of Charlie Tobin, killed in action at Bagnara. (Sid Payne)

39. Fighting from a ditch at Termoli. (Sid Payne)

40. Graves of men killed when a shell struck their truck. (Sid Payne)

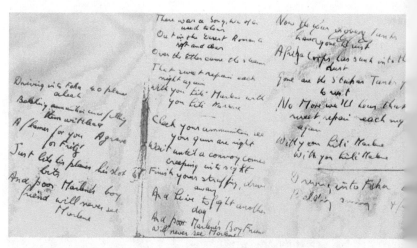

41. The first draft of the song of the regiment. (John Menown)

42. Various SAS badges. (All author)

The first badge for
SPECIAL AIR SERVICE
designed by Coporal TAIT.

CAP BADGE
made in ENGLAND

Winged EXCALIBUR
(King Arthurs sword)
Red, white and Cambridge blue
threads on a Oxford blue shield.

Later badge for
SPECIAL AIR SERVICE

Official stamped EGYPTIAN
CAP BADGE.

Stony, pebbly beach
by groves. No exits for vehicles. Water offshore suitable for landingcraft (approx.) 8–10ft at 25
Rocky headland with conspicuous tower
Believed sand and shingle beach average width 50'–70' backed by Corniche road in front of town and point, and by walled-in groves elsewhere. Vehicle exits as shown. Water offshore believed suitable for all L.C's.
BAGNARA
Coastline made of block and boulder faced railway embankment. Exits for Infantry only, water approx. 5'0" at 50" offshore
Concrete blocks
Barracks

43. Bagnara map. (Author)

Bar to D.S.O.   Captain (Temp. Major) R.B. Mayne.

OPERATION : SICILY. July 10th and 12th. Major R.B.
Mayne carried out two successful operations.
1st.   Capture and destruction of battery on Cape Di
Porco, the outcome of which was vital to safe landing of
a corps. By nightfall the Raiding Squadron which he
commanded had captured 3 additional batteries, 450
prisoners, as well as killing 2 - 300 Italians.
2nd.   Capture and holding of town of Augusta. Landing
was carried out in daylight, a most hazardous combined
operation. By the audacity displayed the Italians were
forced from their positions and masses of most valuable
stores and equipment was saved from enemy demolition.
In both these operations it was Major Mayne's courage,
determination and superb leadership which proved the key t
success. He personally led the men from the landing
craft, in the face of heavy machine gun fire, and in the
case of Augusta raid - mortar fire. By this action he
succeeded in forcing his way to ground where it was
possible to form up and sum up enemy defences.

44. Citation for 2nd DSO. (Author)

45. Disbandment letter sent
to Mike Calvert. (Author)

46. R.B. Mayne in the desert. (Author)

47. R.B. Mayne in his Royal Ulster Rifles uniform. (Author)

48. Captured coastal guns, Capo Murro De Porco. (Muirhead)

49. Captured coastal guns, Capo Murro De Porco. (Both Muirhead)

50. Sgt Christopher O'Dowd, KIA Termoli. (O'Dowd)

51. Pte Dennis James. (James)

52. Duncan Ridler. (Ridler)

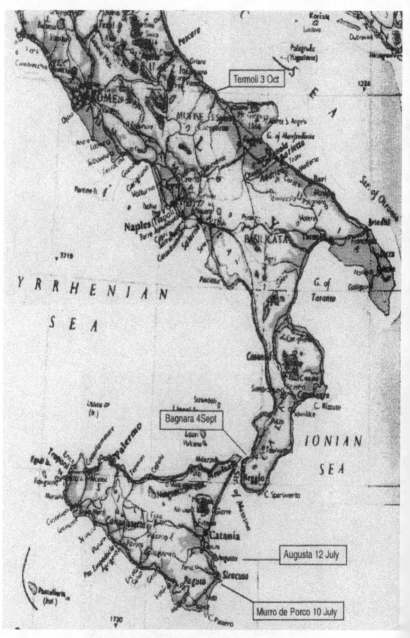

Termoli 3 Oct

Bagnara 4Sept

Augusta 12 July

Murro de Porco 10 July

53. Italy and Sicily map. (Author)

54. Jack Nixon and Jack Leech in commando days. (Nixon)

55. *Ulster Monarch* resupplying. (Author)

COMBINED OPERATIONS HEADQUARTERS,

IA, RICHMOND TERRACE,

WHITEHALL, S.W.I

Telephone :
Whitehall 9777.

28th August, 1945.

My dear Paddy,

I feel I must drop you a line just to tell you how very deeply I appreciate the great honour of being able to address, as my friend, an officer who has succeeded in accomplishing the practically unprecedented task of collecting no less than four D.S.O's.   (I am informed that there is another such superman in the Royal Air Force.)

You deserve all and more, and, in my opinion, the appropriate authorities do not really know their job.   If they did they would have given you a V.C. as well.

Please do not dream of answering this letter, which brings with it my sincerest admiration and a deep sense of honour in having, at one time, been associated with you.

Yours ever,

Bob Laycock.

Lieutenant-Colonel P. Mayne, D.S.O., M.C.,
1st S.A.S. Regiment,
HALSTEAD,
Essex.

56. Bob Laycock letter. The letter was addressed to P. Mayne; perhaps he thought Paddy was short for 'Patrick'? Also, he mistakenly added MC after the DSO. (Author)

57. Sgt C. McEvoy, L/Cpl Fassam and Pte J. Buckley. (Buckley)

58. *Ulster Monarch*. (Author)

59. S/Sgt A.R. Seekings. (Author)

60. Training for rock scaling. (McDougall)

61. SAS Battle Honours. (Author)

62. Lt Col Mayne sits among his men at the disbandment of the SAS. (Author)

63. Sicily. (Author)

64. R.B. Mayne's funeral in Newtownards. (Both *The Newtownards Chronicle*)

65. This image of Blair Mayne in the desert was painted by Jack Courier. Cpl George Howard from the Survey Section GHQ of the Long Range Desert Group always carried this with him in the form of a Christmas card. He said that he always felt safe when he had it with him. (Nigel Howard)

Chapter IX

Termoli: The Hardest Battle

At 5.00 p.m. on 6 September 1943 the Squadron disembarked at Messina and moved into billets on the nearby mole. The following day was spent in re-organising men and equipment in No.2 Troop and B Section of No.1 Troop while everyone was able to catch up with news from home as a mail delivery had been made. Any news from family and friends, however late, was important and provided a welcome break in routine, especially as many had not seen home soil for well over three years. Their stay at Messina was to be brief; they packed up their kitbags and moved out at noon on the 8th with the subsequent six days being spent moving to and from yet more temporary campsites at Gallico, Valencia Porto, Pizza and Scalea. At each location the Squadron's day-to-day life carried on as usual with much time being taken up by the more mundane, but much needed, jobs of re-arming and re-fitting the sections. Despite the constant upheaval of these unsettled conditions the routine of army life had to continue.

Some wounded returned from the various aid stations while other men were posted back to their parent units.

On 8 September the news filtered through to the Squadron that Italy had surrendered. Her remaining forces were to be considered as co-belligerents of the Allies; Italy would later be considered as an ally. Orders were issued to the British forces that senior Italian officers were to be afforded the privilege of their ranks and saluted at all times. Paddy Mayne left his men in no doubt just what would happen to them if he ever caught them adhering to such orders. General Montgomery was said to have regarded the action of his new found allies as 'the biggest double cross in history'.

Meanwhile, the Italian dictator Benito Mussolini had been spirited far away by Italian military police to a ski resort at Gran Sasso in the Apennine mountains. They were obviously hoping to keep him far away from his so-called German friends. However, SS General Otto Skorzeny had some very different ideas and, on 12 September, pulled off a daring rescue mission; by the 13th Mussolini was, for the time being, safe in the German city of Munich with his Nazi allies. It was an incredible operation that must have rankled greatly with the men of the Special Air Service since such a task would have been right up their street. It was not the first time that they had felt that way; as far back as November 1941 David Stirling had said that his men to whom he referred, even at that early stage, as the 'Professionals', should have been used to try to capture General Erwin Rommel instead of the brave, but ill fated, attempt made by a group of commandos drawn from the remains of Layforce. Although Stirling felt that not only would the SAS have captured the legendary German commander, but they would also have ensured that he was where he was said to have been in the first place, it is difficult to see how he could justify this argument since the same flawed intelligence would have been used for an SAS mission. It is also worth remembering that the SAS had an involvement in the planning of the raid in which Lieutenant-Colonel Geoffrey Keyes lost his life. Keyes had briefly been the commanding officer of Paddy Mayne's former unit, No.11 (Scottish) Commando, but there had been a stormy relationship between the two young men who had even come to blows. Keyes was posthumously awarded the Victoria Cross for his actions during the raid.

Many Special Air Service men who fought through the desert campaign came to respect and admire Rommel greatly. This was also true throughout Eighth Army. Rommel was regarded as a soldier who, like themselves, understood how war should be conducted and therefore they considered him as possibly the best overall commander in the field at that time. That admiration even stretched as far as London and Prime Minister Winston Churchill who, on hearing the news of Rommel's death in late 1944, paid tribute to him in the House of Commons. (It was also widely believed in the SAS that Rommel had refused to obey Hitler's infamous Commando order in North Africa. [For details of the Commando Order, see Chapter I.])

During the morning of 16 September Mayne received new orders for the Squadron and they began preparing for an operation that would involve them assisting a Special Service Brigade in the Salerno bridgehead. The raiders were ready for more action with many becoming anxious since they felt that they had been sitting around for long enough. The remainder of the afternoon of the 16th was spent waiting for the move to begin, but their wait was in vain; at 5.00 p.m. news of the cancellation of the operation reached them. However, due to the advances being made by Allied forces, they were soon off on their travels again. Over the next two weeks the Squadron moved to camp-sites at Catania, Canizzaro, Bari, Taranto, Brindisi and then, finally, Manfredonia. Despite these disruptions, and the many logistical problems caused by them, the soldiers' spirits remained high as they continued training. But, as always, they made time for rest and to sample a few bottles of the local vino. Many would have been very well aware of the old army saying 'When you're marching you're not fighting'.

During the early evening of 1 October the raiders boarded their landing craft on which they spent an une-ventful night. Their numbers had been depleted greatly over the last few months and the Squadron's overall strength totalled only 207. At noon on 2 October they embarked from Manfredonia on the start of a seventy-five to eighty-mile sea journey that was expected to last about fourteen hours. They were in the company of another five landing craft infantry (LCIs), which in turn were towing seven LCAs and an LCS. These craft carried the men from Nos 3 (Army) Commando and 40 (Royal Marine) Commando. (In November 1944 the Special Service Brigades were redesignated Commando Brigades, thus eliminating the unfortunate abbreviation of SS brigades. The commanding SS Group was also redesignated as the Commando Group.) The three units formed a Special Service Brigade and their move was timed to coincide with the start of Operation DEVON. The Squadron's primary objectives were to make a sea-borne landing and then advance on the port of Termoli on Italy's Adriatic coast. If both the landing and initial move were achieved successfully they would continue through the eastern side of the town to secure the two bridges over the Biferno river.

Termoli's importance lay in its value to the German Viktor line. The town was the left flank anchor for that line, a forward element of the Gustav line fortifications in the east. Should the Germans hold on to Termoli, the Allied armies – Fifth (US) and Eighth (British) – would have had much extended lines of intercommunication as the lateral road, Highway 87, would have remained in enemy hands. Taking Termoli also offered the possibility of cutting Highway 16 and the retreat of elements of the German forces. The loss of the Viktor line would put pressure on the Germans right across the peninsula to Naples and force them to withdraw to the next defensive line to avoid being outflanked.

Termoli was held by garrison troops and some elements of 1st Fallschirmjäger (Parachute) Division[1], which had been falling back before 78th (Battleaxe) Division.[2] It was estimated that the Termoli garrison was composed only of a detachment of railway construction engineers and a platoon of Fallschirmjäger, the parent battalion of which was defending along the Biferno to the west. In all there were about 600 German troops in the town, formed as a battlegroup. The flexibility of German training allowed effective battlegroups to be extemporised from even the most unlikely combinations of troops, including rear echelon soldiers.

Allied intelligence was uncertain of the whereabouts of 16th Panzer Division, which had been involved against Fifth Army in the Salerno bridgehead where it had sustained heavy casualties. The division had been withdrawn to refit and re-organise but, as soon as Field Marshal Kesselring, the German commander-in-chief in southern Italy, became aware of the British attack on Termoli, it was ordered to move across the country to the left flank. However, some four hours after he had ordered it to move, Kesselring discovered that 16th Panzer had not even begun its journey. General von Vietinghoff, commanding Tenth Army, had not shared Kesselring's sense of urgency and it took a fresh order from the latter to get the division moving. When it did so the move was piecemeal. Two battlegroups – *Kampfgruppen* Stempel and von Döring – eventually arrived at Termoli on 4 October after a ninety-five-mile march over the mountains. Their presence was first detected by a patrol of B Squadron of 56th Reconnaissance Regiment which captured a despatch rider, who was then identified as belonging to 16th Panzer, and then spotted Panzers on Highway 87.

The Allied plan to seize Termoli allowed for a *coup de main* attack from the sea by the Special Service Brigade, who would hold the town until 11 Brigade arrived by land. Artillery and armour would also use the overland route. Following up the Special Service Brigade would be 36 Brigade, who would help consolidate the position. Finally, the Irish Brigade would also come in by sea but, by then, it was expected that all would be secure and Brigadier Nelson Russell, the Irish commander, was told that his move by sea would be like 'a pleasant peacetime cruise' with fighting unlikely for two weeks or so. But the weather, and the presence of 16th Panzer Division, combined to create a very different situation.

At 2.45 a.m. on 3 October the signal for the Special Service Brigade to begin landing was made from the beach by men of No.3 Commando. Since their commanding officer, Major Peter Young, had been wounded in an earlier action and hospitalised, they were under the temporary command of Captain Arthur G Komrower (awarded the Distinguished Service Order for his actions at Termoli) who was acutely aware that his unit was very much under strength, now deploying no more than 180 all ranks. (The brigade totalled no more than 1,000 men. An infantry brigade at full strength might have had some 2,300 men but could deploy only some 1,500 rifles in the line.) But despite this, No.3 Commando had still been assigned the dangerous and difficult job of being the first troops ashore and forming a bridgehead on the beach. As it made its final approach, the landing craft carrying the Raiding Squadron ran aground on a sandbank some fifty yards offshore from the mouth of the Biferno. However, the navy had planned ahead and brought along three smaller assault craft. Nonetheless, the raiders still faced the dangerous job of transferring their equipment in pitch darkness. Major Mayne, never one to panic in any circumstances, boarded the nearest of the three craft and began overseeing the tricky operation. Speed and silence were the top priorities but they also had to ensure that their ammunition and weapons were kept as dry as possible. With the transfer complete, the Squadron continued inshore towards the landing sites.

The night sky was pitch black and a fine mizzle was falling. The beach was very narrow and as the Squadron landed alongside the men from No.40 (RM) Commando many ran the risk of becoming disoriented. The adrenalin was flowing and, if not handled properly, the situation might quickly have turned into one of utter confusion. Sergeant Jock Campbell, from Alex Muirhead's Mortar Platoon, was one of the first to reach the beach. Well briefed and knowing what the situation required, he defied the difficult conditions and took control immediately, moving calmly through the various groups, pushing and harrying everyone around him to move forward as fast as possible. Campbell's actions were not only swift but also decisive and seen by many as instrumental in the rapid deployment of the 3-inch mortar teams, which were ready to come into action as dawn broke.

The marines of No.40 Commando, who were also to take part in the capture of the town, had moved off the beach very quickly and reached a nearby crossroads where they formed up and started their advance. Everything was strangely quiet as the Raiding Squadron moved off the beach and advanced to the top of a nearby ridge, passing quickly through the beachhead formed by No.3 Commando and over the Termoli–Vasto road. Having reached that position unhindered, the raiders stopped for a few minutes to regroup and reform. The Squadron was then divided into its various troops and sections, which began to move out towards their designated objectives. No.3 Troop started a move that would take them across country towards the Termoli–Campomarino road. At the same time No.2 Troop moved on roughly the same bearing but slightly behind them and over to the north of No.3.

At 5.30 a.m. B Section of No.3 Troop, under Lieutenant John Tonkin, spotted their first enemy troops of the day, a small group of Germans who, rather than attacking, appeared to be trying to find cover in a ditch close to a bridge. They were easily captured. At much the same time the Section's mortar team was also about to make its first contact. The team engaged a small enemy convoy of five trucks that were moving slowly and thus made easy targets for the experienced mortarmen. Their first few rounds hit one of the trucks and set it on fire. As soldiers tried to make their escape from the vehicles, one officer was hit and killed and another wounded. A further three Germans simply raised their hands in surrender. The Section had just started to reform after this short action when voices were heard from their flank. More German soldiers had been sighted and an immediate attack was launched on them. Heavy and accurate fire from the Section's Bren gunners soon made short work of the Germans, causing them to flee in total disarray taking their wounded comrades with them. Tonkin, pleased with the outcome of the first few actions, quickly reassembled his men and had them on the move again.

They now knew that there was much activity in the area and so made their way cautiously into what appeared to be a deserted farmyard. Suddenly, the early morning silence was shattered again as they came under a heavy volley of concentrated fire from enemy soldiers in the farm buildings. The mortars were brought into action quickly to try to silence the Germans or force them out of their concealed positions. Despite reacting very swiftly and fiercely, the raiders soon found themselves under a hail of heavy fire from a small field gun as well as numerous small arms. Unsure of the exact strength of the force opposing them, Tonkin made a snap decision and ordered his Section to withdraw from the farmyard to take up defensive positions in the ditch that had just been cleared out. Even as they retraced their steps, the Germans continued to pour heavy and accurate fire on them. Dawn was beginning to break and the small group of men suddenly found that they were totally out of luck. They had been completely boxed in. Unwittingly, they had allowed themselves to be caught in a very dangerous trap and now found themselves facing not only the Germans who had attacked them as they entered the farmyard but also another group of enemy soldiers who had just arrived. Initially, the new arrivals had not been keen to become involved in a fight and it appeared that their only intention had been to make good their escape from Termoli. But when the two German groups combined, it became clear to John Tonkin and his men that they were totally outnumbered as well as outgunned.

Faced with such overwhelming odds, Tonkin reluctantly gave the only order that he considered appropriate: 'Every man for himself.' Tonkin's one real hope was that, somehow, his men would be able to fight their way through the surrounding German troops in ones or twos and then regroup farther inland. With the tables now suddenly turned in their favour, the Germans seized the initiative and closed in on the ditch. However, they appeared to be in no hurry to launch an attack. Perhaps they realised that they had only to wait for the surrounded soldiers to make the next move. But the men of B Section were not prepared to wait for anyone. Almost as soon as they tried to break out of the ditch they became heavily engaged with the large enemy group surrounding them. Lance-Corporal Joe Fassam checked his weapon carefully before standing up and heaving himself over the edge of the ditch. Immediately he came face to face with some of the waiting Germans. But, despite the fact that he was on his own and hopelessly outnumbered, he appeared to have no intention of surrendering or allowing himself to be captured. It seemed to his comrades that he intended to fight his way out of the trap and make good his escape. On clearing the ditch, he fired a long burst at the closest group of Germans. Sadly for him, the odds were just too great and he failed in his brave attempt for freedom. Joe Fassam made very little ground before he fell mortally wounded after being cut down by a fierce volley of fire. However, in the confusion that followed his attempted breakout, six men of the Section were lucky enough to make good their escape. Showing a total disregard for the danger facing them, they even took with them the prisoners who had been captured earlier.

John Tonkin, with the remainder of his section, some twenty-two men in total, was eventually run to ground and captured. Their captors turned out to be some very experienced and battle hardened troops from the German 1st Parachute Division who escorted their unwilling prisoners westwards across country to Guglionesi.

Staff Sergeant Clarke, on seeing that at least a few men had managed to escape, acted immediately and stepped into the breach. He took charge of the remaining raiders and together they fought off the German soldiers who were making menacing advances towards them. Although the odds were stacked heavily against them, their swift action in confronting their attackers forced the latter to move back and give up some vital ground. Shortly after that brief and very fierce firefight, Clarke was struck in the head by a piece of flying shrapnel, but, like many others, he refused to go back for medical treatment. Ignoring the pain that his wound was causing him he continued to push everyone forward. He had no set plan but his intentions were quite simple: to lead his men out of their very precarious position.

The situation was extremely dangerous and was being made even harder for Staff Sergeant Clarke by the fact that some of his men had started suffering very badly from shellshock. The level of enemy activity was continuing to increase all around them and they were still being subjected to a heavy fusillade of German machine-gun fire. Meanwhile the men from A Section, on hearing the firing coming from B Section's position, began to make an advance down through the ditch. They had covered only a short distance before being engaged by a large concentration of enemy troops who obviously knew the route that the Section would take and just where to concentrate their fire. Two men of the Section were hit and wounded during the subsequent heavy fighting. But the casualties inflicted on the German attackers proved to be even heavier: five killed, four wounded and nine captured.

Among the wounded was Captain Bob Melot, the Intelligence Officer, who at the age of 54 (his official age is listed as 49) was by far the oldest man in the Squadron. Private Ralphs, acting on his own initiative, moved forward, running across open ground with his Bren gun at the ready. He managed to find a fairly good position from where he laid down some accurate covering fire, which allowed Lance-Sergeant Goldsmith, who had been in charge of another sub-section, the breathing space to attend to the needs of the wounded soldiers and help evacuate them back to an aid post. Captain Melot, who was Belgian by birth, was an old hand at the art of war and had seen service as a fighter pilot during the Great

War. He wanted to be involved in the fighting and had no time to waste waiting for treatment and so, at the earliest possible opportunity, and with his arm resting in a hastily applied sling, he returned to the action. Private Ralphs would again show great courage later in the day when, as a runner for the Squadron, he carried vital information back and forth across the open ground during the heavy and sustained fighting west of Termoli. Ralphs was acutely aware that each time he was sent out with a new message he would be coming under constant threat from enemy fire but, despite the obvious danger to his life, he never questioned his orders.

After this brief but fierce contact, A Section continued to move cautiously down through the ditch and on towards one of the two bridges. They came across some of the weapons and equipment that had been discarded when the men of John Tonkin's section had been surrounded and captured.

Also at 5.30 a.m. No.1 Troop had reached the Termoli–Campomarino road to begin their advance towards Campomarino. The Troop was moving forward cautiously and, as they approached a slight bend in the road, they suddenly spotted a small tracked motorcycle-type vehicle. It was a K1 Mk101 with a small 10.5mm gun in tow. Although surprised, the leading raiders reacted quickly and opened fire on the vehicle as it neared the bend. The crew were killed instantly and the gun was put out of action. No.1 Troop moved forward again and, as they rounded the bend, many of them looked on in total disbelief as they witnessed what happened next. For some strange reason a few German soldiers had watched them coming and left their defensive positions at the roadside

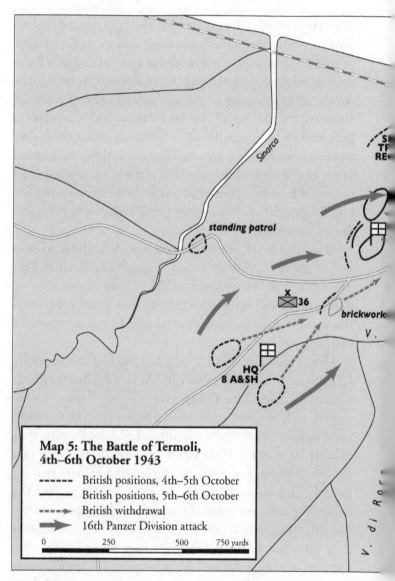

Map 5: The Battle of Termoli, 4th–6th October 1943

------ British positions, 4th–5th October

——— British positions, 5th–6th October

- - - ▸ British withdrawal

➤ 16th Panzer Division attack

| 0 | 250 | 500 | 750 yards |

The Battle of Termoli

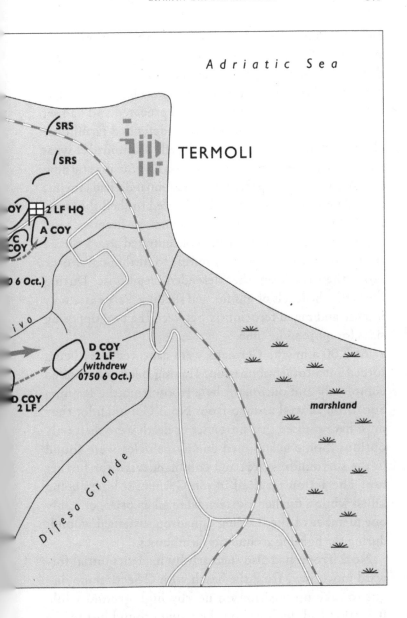

Adriatic Sea

TERMOLI

SRS

SRS

OY 2 LF HQ

A COY

C
COY

0 6 Oct.)

i v o

D COY
2 LF
(withdrew
0750 6 Oct.)

D COY
2 LF

marshland

Difesa Grande

before moving towards the raiders with hands raised in surrender. But their countrymen seemed to take a very different view of events as they opened fire on their own men as well as the soldiers of the approaching troop. The Germans were obviously very well prepared and had set up a fortified position in a heavily defended farmhouse close to the bend. Despite being briefly astounded at what had just happened, the raiders wasted no time in returning fire. A forward group from No.3 Commando had also just moved up into the area and they started to shell the farmhouse with their 4-inch mortars. The sheer firepower and accuracy of this combined and concentrated attack forced the Germans to make a hasty retreat to further cover back down the road in another defended farmhouse. During the battle the levels of gunfire and shelling were extremely intense and raged ferociously between the two opposing sides for quite some time.

At 7.00 a.m. the Germans were captured after being forced into total submission. Having been surrounded completely and outfought by a troop from the Raiding Squadron as well as men from No.3 Commando, they must have realised that surrender or death were their only options. Some abandoned enemy vehicles were found in the surrounding area and commandeered for further use. The action resulted in ten German soldiers being killed while a further fourteen were taken prisoner. Only one member of the Raiding Squadron sustained wounds during the fighting around the farmhouses.

No.2 Troop had also successfully made its initial forward move away from the beach with C Section moving out to take up position on nearby high ground while B Section had deployed on the rising ground just to the east of a road junction. However, shortly after arriving, C Section and its mortar detachment had been spotted and came under enemy fire. The Germans had taken over and fortified some nearby farm buildings for their heavy machine guns and were laying down concentrated fire from there. The mortar crews and Bren gunners lost no time in locating their targets and soon ranged in with accurate and devastating fire that silenced all the enemy guns and allowed the buildings, and nine German soldiers inside, to be captured.

C Section remained in position at the captured farm buildings until, at 9.00 a.m., they were ordered to make another forward move. This time the Section was to take up new positions on the higher ground just west of another recently captured farmhouse. By late morning all members of the Squadron had engaged the enemy and were moving closer to their objectives of the two bridges and the town of Termoli. The remaining men of No.3 Troop began moving down the Campomarino road heading towards the rail and road bridge to take up new positions where they made contact with a small group of soldiers from the advancing elements of 11 Brigade.

No.1 Troop, led by C Section, had just started an advance down the Termoli–Larino road towards one of the bridges. During the initial planning stages for the operation it had been hoped that this could have been captured intact but, as the raiders approached, they saw that they had arrived too late. The bridge looked as though it had been demolished only recently. Despite the very obvious signs of heavy enemy activity in the area, the Troop could locate no German soldiers and so stopped and set up all-round defensive positions.

At 1.00 p.m. the men of A Section of No.2 Troop spotted approximately 200 German soldiers who were attempting to move to the south along a track in the Difesa Grande. The mortar crews sited at No.40 (RM) Commando's position had also spotted these troops and opened fire. The Royal Marine mortarmen's fire was very accurate and they hit and destroyed an enemy tracked vehicle. Once the firing had stopped, a small recce patrol was sent forward to investigate the results of the shelling. It returned a short time later to report finding only one wounded German soldier. The shelling had been successful as his comrades had obviously dispersed and gone to ground.

While moving towards the town, the men of B Section came into contact with another group of marines from No. 40 Commando. After a short discussion, it was decided that, given the lack of information on enemy strength, it might be beneficial for all concerned if they joined forces. Having formed up they began patrolling carefully towards San Giacomo but had not made much progress when one of their signallers received an urgent radio transmission. The message ordered them to begin an immediate withdrawal as the area they were moving through was about to be shelled. There was no need for the signal to be repeated as no one had any great desire to be caught in a bombardment, especially from their own guns. The small group of soldiers began moving hurriedly to the east and once well out of the danger area set up all-round defensive positions and remained out of sight until early the following morning.

It was becoming very obvious to everyone that large numbers of German troops had been deployed around Termoli, as there had been a very noticeable increase in their levels of activity and resistance since the landings. C Section had just started a westward move towards the head of a ditch when they observed a group of enemy soldiers who were hastily digging in on a ridge about 800 yards west of San Giacomo. It was decided that the Section should move into a wood where they would have a better vantage point and it was also hoped that this move would afford them better protection. From the cover provided by the trees they would also be able to observe and supply more information on enemy movements. It proved to be a good move; they were able to watch as some German motorcycle despatch riders moved back and forward between the pillboxes on the road to Guglionesi.

In roughly the same area as the pillboxes, they spotted what appeared to be the outline of a German fighter aircraft that had been camouflaged very roughly and looked as though it might recently have been damaged in a crash. Derrick Harrison ordered four of his men, Bob McDougall, Darkie Rogerson, Paddy Kenna and Bob Seekings, to carry out two-man reconnaissance patrols to determine the strength and movements of the enemy forces. The patrol of McDougall and Rogerson was successful as they managed to observe a large number of German troops taking up new positions and digging in hastily. Both men knew that there was no time to lose, as their information was vitally important. As they made their return journey, they met up with some men of 2nd Lancashire Fusiliers, one of the battalions of 11 Brigade (the other two battalions of 11 Brigade were 1st Surreys and 5th Northamptons). Although very pressed for time, Private McDougall felt that the Lancs should also be informed of the mounting danger facing them. He tried to explain what they had just seen but, to his amazement, his warning was brushed aside. Then the Lancs' RSM, obviously not impressed by these two wandering soldiers who appeared to be detached from their unit, intervened and informed his commanding officer that he was going to place them under close arrest. Although taken by surprise, Darkie Rogerson decided that he had heard enough. He stepped forward and explained the situation to the RSM, pulling no punches and making his point while using quite a few words containing no more than four letters. He hoped that, in this way, his message would be understood more easily. However, the two men did not wait long enough to find out if Darkie had been successful and both hastily legged it back to their own positions.

Squadron Headquarter Troop was also on the move and was just approaching a bend in the road. While trying to reach a ditch that ran parallel to the road they came into sudden contact with a party of about forty German soldiers who had mortar support. A very fierce firefight developed but it was the Germans who took the majority of the punishment. Some members of the hard-pressed enemy dragged themselves cautiously out of the ditch and began walking forward with their hands raised in surrender. But yet again, their comrades decided against that option and opened fire on them. Another section from No.40 (RM) Commando had just arrived and together with Headquarter Troop captured the ditch and took all the Germans in it prisoner.

Termoli was already proving to be much more than a raiding operation and the already stiff fighting would continue over the next few days.

Notes

1. In the German forces the parachute forces were part of the *Luftwaffe*
    although they fought regularly under army command. They were
    regarded as some of the finest troops in the German forces and Field
    Marshal Alexander considered them to be the toughest and most
    professional of all German fighting troops.
2. This Division had already fought in Tunisia and Sicily and had gained a
    reputation as one of the finest fighting formations in the Mediterranean
    theatre. Among its achievements was the assault on the mountaintop
    village of Centuripe in Sicily which General Montgomery had described
    as 'impossible'. The brigades that made up the Division were 11, 36 and
    38 (Irish) Brigades while its reconnaissance regiment – 56th – was already
    battle hardened and considered one of the best such units in the Army.

Chapter X

Triumph and Tragedy

In the early evening of 3 October the Raiding Squadron was relieved by 2nd Lancashire Fusiliers and ordered to move back into Termoli where billets were established in the deserted monastery buildings. The Squadron's casualty list for 3 October was one dead (Lance-Corporal Fassam), three wounded (Captain Melot MC, Private O'Gorman and Private Singer) and twenty-two missing. The latter were Lieutenant Tonkin, Sergeants Markham and McEvoy; Lance-Corporals Ainsley, Brundel, Buckley, Cordiner, Cummings, Swann, Vidler and Wood; Privates Asquith, Commerie, Finnimore, Griffiths, Judge, Lea, Masker, McBeth, McDonald, McKenzie and Winn. Reports in the war diary stated that enemy casualties included twenty-three dead, seventeen wounded and thirty-nine captured.

As far as everyone was concerned, Termoli had been captured and the Squadron, having fought hard, had completed its tasks successfully. Its soldiers spent most of the day moving into their new billets in requisitioned houses.

Although feeling very weary they had already begun sorting out weapons and personal equipment in readiness for yet another embarkation as the newly arrived troops of 78th Division were expected to relieve the Special Service Brigade at Termoli.

During the early morning of 4 October Lance-Corporal Duncan Ridler, the Squadron Intelligence Corporal, was detailed to escort several German prisoners back to HQ. He had not gone far before finding himself in serious trouble. Caught in an ambush, he came under close-range fire from five German soldiers. His response was immediate and instinctive but, as he tried to return fire, a round jammed in the breach of his Thompson. Training, experience and the natural instinct for survival took over as he unclipped his last grenade and tossed it into the midst of his attackers. Much to Duncan's obvious relief the explosion had the desired effect as it forced the Germans to take cover behind the nearest bank. Although he did not know it at the time, Lady Luck was almost certainly on his side; two German rounds had gone straight through the front of his beret.

The thought of giving up and allowing himself to be captured did not enter Ridler's mind. Instead, he employed the art of bluff and called out orders to some non-existent comrades. He was delighted, and extremely relieved, to see his ruse work brilliantly. It fooled the Germans into thinking that he had more troops nearby to back him up. Assuming their position to be hopeless, the Germans stood up, dropped their weapons and surrendered. Before they realised what had happened, they were rounded up and escorted back to HQ with the original group of prisoners who had gone to ground when the ambush started. An unexpected bonus for the Intelligence Section was that a weapon carried by one of the German soldiers happened to be one of their latest models, a new type of paratrooper's rifle, the *Fallschirmjägergewehr 42*. A rather relieved Duncan Ridler also discovered that it was the very rifle that not so long before had been responsible for causing the two holes in his beret.

At 5.30 p.m. on 4 October A and C Sections of No.2 Troop and C Section of No.1 Troop, all under command of Major Harry Poat, received orders to move out to new positions along the eastern ridge at Torre Sinacre. Their task was to try to hold a gap that had been identified in the general forward defensive line. Although there were intermittent outbreaks of shelling and air attacks, there were no further threats of enemy activity for the men of the Squadron to worry about throughout the early evening and the night of 4–5 October. However, strong rumours were circulating among all the men billeted in and around Termoli that the Germans were building up to a massive counter-attack. Those rumours would turn out to be well founded as the Germans had sent 16th Panzer Division from the Naples area,[1] where it had been re-organising after the Salerno battles, with orders to re-capture Termoli at all costs.

During the early morning of the 5th levels of enemy activity continued to build up and a large concentration of German soldiers was spotted making preparations on the western ridge near the railway station. Captain Tony Marsh with two sections of No.2 Troop had been sent out to take up a holding position on the right flank. Pressure was beginning to build up and they had come under persistent, heavy shelling from the deadly 88mm anti-aircraft guns deployed in a ground role. These weapons were being supported by heavy mortar and small-arms fire. The situation on the ground around Termoli was beginning to get very serious and, from the skies, about a dozen *Luftwaffe* planes made a determined attack on the harbour area. Marsh was an experienced officer and felt certain that serious trouble was brewing for his men. His position had been tenuous to begin with but was further weakened when he received new orders telling him to withdraw the men of C Section from his defensive line and move them into a nearby wooded area under command of 56th Reconnaissance Regiment. This small wood was being subjected to an intense pounding by some very heavy fire from tanks of 16th Panzer Division. The heavily armoured vehicles were manned by experienced crews, some of whom had seen service on the Russian front, and had broken through on the left flank to put in a strong and dangerous counter-attack. As the Section arrived at their new location they came across a scene of carnage with badly wounded men and the bodies of their dead comrades lying amidst broken and destroyed equipment.

There had been much fighting and the situation was confused, so much so that some of the raiders believed that the Recce men and gunners of the Royal Artillery had run away, abandoning their carriers and anti-tank guns. However, this was not the case. The anti-tank gun detachments had fought their guns to the last and, in the traditions of the Royal Artillery, had not surrendered their weapons. (In the Royal Regiment of Artillery the guns are considered to be the regiment's colours and thus to be defended to the last). One Recce man, Trooper Ives, took over an anti-tank gun, the detachment of which had been killed, and continued to fire at the enemy tanks. He, too, died as he served the gun. As for the carriers, these had not been abandoned but had been laagered on the orders of Lieutenant-Colonel Kendal Chavasse DSO, the commanding officer of 56 Recce. Bren-gun carriers were never intended to fight tanks since they were but lightly armoured and even more lightly armed.

C Section knew almost at once that they could not possibly hold out and defend the position. Thankfully, any decision was taken out of their hands when they received an urgent radio message asking them if they could make another forward move. This new move was to prove yet another hazardous journey. The Section was being asked to try and bring back into action an anti-tank gun to their left. They were expected to make their way through the very heavy shellfire being directed at them by the tanks. Although they completed the move without casualties it had been in vain: when they arrived they found that the gun had already been destroyed. Nothing more could be done so they decided to advance farther down into the valley, hoping that they might reach the dead ground just in front of No.40 (RM) Commando's positions and, perhaps, provide some covering fire throughout the area.

This move appears to have been made without reference to Colonel Chavasse as both 56 Recce and 11 Brigade reported in their post-battle accounts that the SRS section had been overrun. Fortunately, the reconnoitres were able to hold the position against the Panzers until Chavasse's small force was ordered to move back to a firm base provided by 2nd Lancashire Fusiliers. For this action Colonel Chavasse was awarded a Bar to his DSO to become the sole Reconnaissance Corps officer to be so decorated.

After various moves, the men of C Section returned unscathed to rejoin their comrades of A Section who had remained in their original positions. Although still coming under determined attack A Section had been able to hold the Germans. With his two sections reunited, Marsh decided that it was time for another forward move. The enemy gunners were still very active and continued to shell the area heavily as the sections began moving northwards. This was a highly dangerous move during which several men were wounded severely by the blast from a mortar round that landed in their midst. Mortars were deadly when used against infantry units on the battlefield as their rounds fell almost vertically, spreading a deadly swath of shrapnel across a wide radius.

Lance-Corporal Sid Payne stopped to administer some basic first aid to the wounded. After dealing with Dickie Mylor's wounds he crawled over him to reach Lance-Corporal John 'Ginger' Hodgkinson, who had sustained serious damage to his knee from the blast.

> There really was very little that I could possibly do for him as I had no real medical supplies or morphine with me to dull the pain. All that I could offer him was some codeine tablets, and they would be no good to him in his situation.

The only thing that Sid could do was to apply field dressings over the wounds to stem the flow of blood until medical help could be found. Payne was an experienced soldier who had dealt with injured men before so he knew almost at once that Hodgkinson's wounds were very bad and would probably put him out of action for a long time, possibly ending his army service. He was also in no doubt that they would be causing him intense agony. The pain from Ginger's injuries was so great that it had reduced him to begging and shouting for someone to show him some mercy. The others knew that he wanted one of them to put an end to his suffering. However, that was the kind of request they could not contemplate granting.

It was imperative that Ginger be moved to cover at once but he was a big man and it would be difficult to shift him quickly. Any movement would be highly dangerous as they were still under heavy enemy fire. Thankfully, a two-wheeled wooden farm cart was found nearby and was used to carry him, with the other casualties brought along behind. Everyone was very aware of the danger of being hit again but had no choice other than to continue moving towards the beach. But the necessity of taking their wounded men with them was slowing everything down. The Germans, although still not totally aware of what was happening, had increased the severity and accuracy of their shelling. Sid Payne knew that there was nothing he could do but try to keep as low to the ground as possible and hope for the best. 'The German gunners were throwing every type of shell that they had at us but thankfully the ground was pretty soft and it was taking some of the force out of the explosions.'

The bombardment had reached such a fearsome level that it had forced the depleted sections to abandon any thoughts of further progress and look for cover. (It seemed that the position of the British forces around Termoli was becoming very precarious as the weather was assisting the enemy by not only preventing the movement across the Biferno of the main body of 78th Division with its armour and artillery support, but also grounding the tactical aircraft that might have supported the Special Service Brigade.) The only suitable cover that could accommodate everyone was a culvert about 900 yards east of one of the bridges; but it was far from ideal as it was just some 150 yards from the enemy lines. Before very long the German gunners found their range again and pinned what remained of the two sections down with even more intensive shelling. Shortly after taking shelter in the culvert they were startled to discover that they were not the only fugitives there; it was full of some very frightened Italians who had also been seeking refuge. Unable to make any further progress due to the intensity of the bombardment, they decided that their best plan was to wait for darkness before attempting any further moves. Lieutenant Harrison realised that their situation had become very serious and decided to send Lance-Corporal Payne to try to locate the CO. He hoped that some reinforcements and medics could be sent to help them. On finding Major Mayne, Sid was told to go and inform the other units in the area of the situation. Before very long he managed to find some senior officers but was not really certain if they believed what he was trying to tell them. A Regimental Sergeant Major was sent out with him to verify his story. The two men had not walked very far when a shell exploded close to them. Sid instinctively ducked at the sound of the explosion but the RSM reacted quite differently and dived headlong through the open door of the nearest building. Sid had seen enough and headed back to find his own section again.

Back in the culvert, a quick head count revealed that several men were missing from the sections; it was thought that they had disappeared during the move down to the culvert. Meanwhile, four men who had been caught and wounded in the mortar blast were in a very serious condition while it was discovered that John Hodgkinson had also sustained serious shrapnel wounds to his back. Sadly, these injuries had not been spotted in the initial rush to get him under cover and it was almost certainly these wounds that proved fatal. He died in the culvert before he could receive medical attention.

When darkness fell, the two battered and depleted sections were able finally to make their way back along the beach where they met up with some more of their own men under Harry Poat. Doors had to taken from shattered houses and used as makeshift stretchers for the wounded. Bob McDougall and three other men were given the task of carrying the wounded back towards the town and an aid post. The weight of the men and the cumbersome wooden doors hampered the stretcher-bearers greatly but they continued very cautiously down some dark and narrow streets. All four were extremely tense and nervous because they knew that they would make easy targets should the Germans take them by surprise. Progress was fairly slow as they were watching carefully for any movement. Their caution proved worthwhile as, suddenly, the dull glint of a gun barrel was seen in an open window. The barrel began turning ominously towards Bob McDougall. He had kept his Bren slung around his neck and was the first to react to the threat. Pulling hard on the trigger and firing from the hip, he emptied a full magazine through the window. He did not stop to find out who had been on the other side of the window. Bob knew that in action you might get one chance only and could not afford to hesitate: 'Anything at all that moved or even showed its head above grass level you just shot at.' Thankfully, nothing else was encountered throughout the rest of the journey and they delivered the casualties safely to an aid post. With their wounded comrades in safe hands, they set off to rejoin their comrades on the beach. In spite of receiving urgent treatment from the medical staff, nothing could be done for one of the men they had left behind. Private B. McLaughlan had also suffered some very severe wounds from the mortar round which proved fatal; he died on 12 October.

When he returned to his section it came as a welcome surprise for Bob McDougall to find that Paddy Mayne had arrived to take control.

> It was normal practice with him; he was never idle and was either helping, pushing or instructing everyone around or near him. On more than one occasion they were not even his own men but that did not matter to Paddy. They just received some simple words of kindness or encouragement.

Termoli was beginning to come under a fierce bombardment of heavy and accurate fire from 88mm guns, tanks and mortars as the battle-hardened enemy soldiers began to mount some very strong counter-attacks. No.1 Troop was ordered to move out at once as the situation was worsening. At much the same time the remainder of the Squadron, consisting of the men from No.3 Troop and B Section of No.2 Troop, about sixty in all, had been resting in the monastery when they received urgent orders to move out and take up southward facing defensive positions in the ditch that ran alongside the nearby road. It was hoped that they would be able to counter any possible attacks that might be put in from their left flank.

Five trucks had been lined up in a narrow walled street near the monastery to take No.1 Troop forward to their new positions. Most men had just finished packing their fighting kit and were boarding the waiting vehicles when a shell suddenly came hurtling down and scored a direct hit. It landed right in the middle of one of the packed trucks and exploded amongst the soldiers who had been carrying a large quantity of detonators, grenades and ammunition in their packs and belts. The resulting explosion had a terrifying and devastating effect in such a confined space. A hail of enemy shells continued landing all around the area but luckily the majority missed their targets and landed in the soft soil, which resulted in the force of the explosions being dampened slightly. The remainder of the troop who had not suffered injuries from the blast showed a total disregard for the falling shells as they ran towards the lorry to help.

However, the situation facing them was totally hopeless and there was little or nothing they could do for many of their friends. No training could have prepared them for the horrific sights they were about to witness. As they neared what remained of the truck they were met with a scene that resembled a butcher's shop. In seconds, the small street and surrounding area had become a bloodbath. Pieces of flesh and body parts hung from nearby telephone wires or drooped from the branches of overhanging trees. The rescuers had to fight with their own thoughts and emotions as they battled through the carnage. It must have been very difficult to avoid being violently sick, crying or just turning and running away from such butchery. A family of innocent civilians who had been standing watching as the soldiers left had been caught up in the terrifying explosion and was blown into little pieces. The acrid smoke hanging over the area began to clear very slowly but a terrible sickly smell that was a mixture of cordite, blood and burnt flesh lingered heavily in the air. Corporal David Danger was one of the first to arrive on the scene of the tragedy. He had sheltered from the blast in a doorway and counted himself lucky because another man who had been sheltering alongside him had sustained shrapnel wounds to both legs. As he reached the remains of the lorry he found one man staggering wildly around and holding both hands to his head.

> He was obviously in extreme agony and screaming uncontrollably, 'What about my eyes, what about my eyes?' There was blood gushing heavily from a severe head wound and one eye was hanging out of its socket and lying on his cheek.

Corporal Danger paused to regain his composure, took a deep breath, swallowed hard, and told the terrified man that everything would be all right. 'I knew almost instinctively from looking at his injuries that they were very serious but in all honesty I just didn't have the heart to tell him the awful truth.' Jack Nixon, who had been attending to a call of nature on the other side of the wall when the explosion happened, found it very hard to come to terms with what was in front of him. 'Mixed in with the wreckage and bodies of our lads were the remains of a family of Italians who did some washing for us; they were gutted and spread everywhere.'

Private Douglas Monteith, who had been standing close to the parked lorries, was picked up like a small rag doll by the force of the blast and slammed backwards into a wall. The impact was so severe that it hammered his helmet down onto his head and knocked him unconscious. As he started slowly to recover some of his battered senses, he groped around and found himself covered in blood.

But thank God I had not been injured at all and in the end turned out to be one of the luckier ones as the blood wasn't really mine. It belonged to Skin [Major Bill Fraser] who had also suffered injuries and was lying on top of me.

Monty had indeed managed to survive the blast and escape with his life. However, due to the effects of concussion he was admitted to 70th General Hospital.

The bodies, with the casualties and walking wounded, were taken back into the monastery and placed under the temporary care of Lance-Sergeant Joe Goldsmith. Although dazed by what had happened, the nuns worked to the best of their abilities to help the injured soldiers but they suffered greatly from a very limited supply of medical necessities. The best that they could offer was to bandage the many wounds. Hard as it must have been for the rest of the men they could not stay and help; their services were required urgently elsewhere.

Fourteen men of No.1 Troop were killed outright by the explosion while a further three died shortly afterwards. The dead were Sergeants Finlay, Henderson, McNinch and O'Dowd; Lance-Corporals Crisp, Grant, McDonald and Sillifants; Privates Cassidy, Davison, Duncan,

Grimster, Hearne, McAlpine, Pocock, Skinner MM and Stewart-Johnson.

Sergeant Reg Seekings had a very narrow escape from almost certain death as he had been just about to board the lorry when the shell landed. He was picked up and thrown backwards by the force of the blast but, somehow, survived the bloody carnage. Despite being badly stunned and shaken he picked himself up and immediately ran back to the lorry to see if he could offer any assistance. Sadly he found that many of his men were beyond help of any kind. The lorry's driver, Sergeant McNinch, was still sitting bolt upright behind the steering wheel and apparently unhurt. Reg wrenched open the door to try and get him out and only then noticed the large piece of metal tubing that had penetrated the back of the cab. It had also gone straight through McNinch, killing him outright and pinning him into position. Somehow, Captain John Wiseman had also miraculously survived the blast and, if possible, had been even more fortunate than Seekings. He had been sitting in the passenger seat next to the driver when the shell landed. Bob Lowson, along with the men from his section, was also one of the fortunate who managed to cheat death. He had led his men out of the monastery and lined them up at the back of the line of trucks. 'For some unexplained reason I was going to be a gentleman and let the other sections board the transport first.' One of the men from his waiting section, Billy Stalker, suddenly stepped forward, leaned on his shoulder and asked: 'And where the Hell do you think you're going?' It was quite probably that simple question that saved all their lives because Bob immediately told them to jump onto the back of the first truck.

Captain Phil Gunn, the Medical Officer, had been called to the scene. He arrived very quickly but the situation for most of the seriously injured was hopeless. Gunn had neither the equipment nor the facilities to deal with wounds of the severity facing him. There have always been some differences of opinion as to how the direct hit came about. Some said that it was an act of God, or just a lucky shot, while others believed it to be the result of controlled or directed enemy fire. There had definitely been an artillery observation post in the church tower in the centre of Termoli. Subsequently, the Irish Brigade identified the location of the observer and an end was put to his activities.

However, many from the Raiding Squadron never had any doubt and to this day maintain that the observer remained in his position for a very long time after they moved out. The shock caused by the large loss of life had a devastating effect on the entire Squadron. Many of the men had served together, having been veterans of the early commando units and the desert campaigns, and were very good friends. They had become a very large but close-knit family. For obvious reasons it was never talked about but it is thought that two men had been so severely wounded in the blast that they had to be put out of their misery.

The explosion had also had a terrible effect on Paddy Mayne who found it an almost soul destroying experience. However, a lot can be gleaned about Mayne's character from one of his many letters home, in which he asked his older sister, Barbara, to visit the mother of Private Canning, one of the injured, a young man from Belfast, some twelve miles from Mayne's own hometown of Newtownards in County Down. Barbara was to tell Private Canning's mother that, although her son had been wounded, he had not been hurt very seriously. Such a request was not just a one-off occurrence as Mayne cared greatly for all the men under his command. Their wives, families, and even some of their sweethearts received letters, although, technically, the latter had no entitlement. Since wartime security conditions required that the letters be censored, families were only given basic information about the welfare of their loved ones.

The Special Raiding Squadron had suffered heavily over the past two days and was a much depleted unit as the remaining men moved out to new positions. However, their ranks were bolstered when some commandos who were supposed to be having a brief rest in the area joined them. Even those men who had been on cooking duty at headquarters were not spared as they were brought out and sent to join the defensive lines. The defences were strengthened further during the early afternoon by the arrival of a 40mm Bofors gun and six anti-tank guns. A short time later, another two anti-tank guns were brought forward and moved quickly into position. It was hoped that those weapons would provide more support and ease some of the mounting pressure on Major Poat.

By 5.30 p.m. the threat to the left flank had noticeably decreased, except for some occasional shelling, and so Headquarter Troop and their mortar section remained at their posts near the railway station. No.3 Troop, with B Section of No.2 Troop, under Captain Lepine, received orders to move across to the right sector to take up new positions between the beach and the railway.

At 7.00 p.m. Harry Poat also moved his men out to take up a new position that would place them in front and to the left of the goods yard. During his move he was extremely

pleased to make contact with some men from 2nd Special
Air Service, commanded by Roy Farran, a fellow country-
man of Paddy Mayne. Farran's squadron had recently been
sent into the Termoli area as the fighting around Taranto
had finished. It was relatively quiet throughout the night
of the 5th and also the early morning of the 6th. There was
only a slight amount of enemy activity to trouble them
and that short respite allowed the men of the Squadron to
have some much needed sleep.

The overall positions at dawn on 6 October were as
follows: a single troop from No.40 Commando with ten
men from the Raiding Squadron were holding positions
between the beach and the cemetery; A Section, No.3
Troop and B Section, No.2 Troop, about thirty men,
and two anti-tank guns were supporting the twenty men
from 2nd SAS who had been ordered to take up positions between the beach and the railway goods yard.
Major Poat along with the remainder of No.2 Troop and
C Section, No.1 Troop were placed in front of the goods
yard with support from two anti-tank guns and an extra
four Sherman tanks that had arrived at dawn. A Canadian
squadron with a further eight Shermans had also taken up
position 800 yards over on their left; these tanks were from
the *Trois Rivières* (Three Rivers) Regiment. The men from
the mortar sections had taken up new positions in a ditch
just to the rear of Captain Lepine's section. Alex Muirhead
received an urgent message informing him that some more
men were waiting to be collected from one of the other
sections that was holding a position farther down the main
road. He ordered Private George Bass to take one of the
captured German lorries and bring them back. Luck played
a large part in the completion of his task, as George had

to drive past a Mk IV tank that had been dug in along the roadside. (Although he identified it as a Tiger this was not so, as 16th Panzer did not deploy any Tigers at Termoli.)

Perhaps the tank crew thought that it was one of their own vehicles considering my direction of travel and its markings. Or maybe they had just simply run out of ammunition because it never even fired a shot at us.

He decided that it would be much wiser not to stay around to find out why and so kept his foot pressed down very hard on the accelerator pedal. George had a truck full of very relieved passengers when they finally reached what they could regard as comparative safety.

Note

1. The Division had served in Russia and had suffered heavily at Stalingrad. It was rebuilt in Germany with a core of survivors from the Russian front and was then deployed to Italy. As noted in the previous chapter, it had taken severe casualties at Salerno from Allied shelling, including bombardment by battleships and was again withdrawn to re-organise with replacement personnel and vehicles. In normal German practice, it fought in *Kampfgruppen*, or battlegroups, at Termoli.

Chapter XI

Counter-attack

The orders issued to the Squadron on the morning of 6 October were for it to stop any further German attacks. If successful, the Squadron's actions would then allow the main force to attempt a push farther inland on the left flank. Weather conditions, bad ever since the initial landing, were by now atrocious, with heavy rainfall causing the rivers to overflow and the lower ground of the coastal area to turn into mud. The defenders dug their slit trenches as deep as they possibly could into the sodden ground, watched over by Mayne, who seemed to be in the right frame of mind for a good fight. Not only had he recently lost many good men but he also knew that he could lose many more in the coming battles. Those present recalled that his face had a look like thunder and his mood was as black as the weather overhead as he walked calmly among his men and made certain that they were aware of his feelings. As he passed their positions, he issued his own very explicit orders for the coming day: 'We came here to take this place, we've taken it and we're staying. What we have we hold on to.'

The battle that followed would prove a most severe test and provide the raiders with some totally new and very hard experiences. The soldiers of the Special Raiding Squadron, by their nature, were more used to being attackers. At 5.00 a.m. the Germans launched their first counter-attack of the day on what was to become known to many of the Squadron as Bren Gun Ridge. There were only about 100 men to defend the ridge but they amassed a total of thirty Brens, added to which was the usual array of small arms, including Thompson sub-machine guns. The second member of each Bren-gun team would be frantically reloading the magazines almost as fast as they were being emptied. Each magazine held a total of thirty rounds of .303 ammunition, although the normal load was twenty-eight, which allowed the gunners to lay down some devastating firepower. This would prove to be one of the decisive factors in the fighting throughout the day, allowing attack after attack to be brought to a standstill and then pushed back. Even when the Germans did get in close, they found that they were being hammered backwards by bullets fired into them from almost point-blank range. The small band of defenders would not yield any ground. Faced with such a determined defence the attackers had no choice other than to keep their heads down and rely heavily on their mortar and sniper fire.

Lance-Corporal Terry Moore received urgent orders to take his radio set over to one of the flanks. Once he had set up and established communications, he was to act as the link between his own men and the commandos to the left

of his section. Even as he was moving he was looking for
the best position from which to establish radio contact.

> The terrain was very open and the only possible shel-
> ter I could see was a rather small, isolated farm building.
> Although it was painted white and, therefore, stuck out
> like a sore thumb, I knew that I had no other choice and
> realised that I would simply have to make it do.

The area surrounding his chosen position was subject to
heavy and sustained enemy fire. Round after round crashed
into the ground throwing shards of deadly shrapnel and
debris into the air. The German gunners were well practised and demonstrating their usual accuracy at long range
with their 88s and mortars. That meant that the small
building continued taking numerous hits.

Before very long Terry Moore knew that he had placed
himself in serious danger of being wounded badly or killed
but he remained at his post and continued to maintain contact. The commando unit, who numbered only about sixty
in total, suffered much heavy punishment with only two of
its number escaping any form of injury during the numerous counter-attacks. Despite the defenders' resolute stand,
one section of Germans managed to make a daring move
forward and took up positions in the nearby cemetery. They
were spotted by one of the four Shermans from 3rd County
of London Yeomanry, which rooted them out with a few
well-aimed rounds. Faced with such dangerous and accurate
fire the Germans withdrew. But they were reluctant to fall
back far and still proved determined to hold onto the ground,
taking cover in some nearby houses and establishing new
firing positions for their mortars and machine guns. Their

presence continued to pose a very serious threat as they laid down fire. C Section of No.1 Troop decided to tackle this problem and opened fire on the houses with an anti-tank gun. The Germans must have felt that they could do no more and finally made a hasty retreat to move back out of range.

Meanwhile Terry Moore was still showing great courage, and complete disregard for his own safety, as he continued to maintain radio communications. 'The pounding from the shells was terrible and at times it was simply just a case of keeping my head down and hoping that the next one didn't have my name on it.' But it was becoming obvious that the Germans had been using his signals as a homing aid; their mortar fire was becoming ever more accurate. At last he received orders to leave the radio set behind and abandon his position immediately. However, he was not finished and his new task would be just as dangerous; he was to act as a runner between the units. Lance-Corporal Moore was too good a soldier to pass up any opportunity and when he came across a German BMW motorcycle complete with sidecar he knew that it would be ideal for delivering orders. The levels of fighting around Termoli had become very fierce and ammunition was being expended very quickly, creating a danger that the Squadron could run out. Paddy Mayne spotted Moore riding back and forward on his motorbike and ordered him to use his transport to locate some fresh supplies. Moore set off to find the nearest supply dump. After travelling only a short distance he reached a crossroads where he found a solitary military policeman with a jeep. Again, he saw an opportunity: 'Ideal for the job in hand and just what I really need,' he thought to himself.

He was familiar with the jeep and knew that he had just found a vehicle capable of carrying even more of the much needed ammunition to his beleaguered comrades. Surprisingly, or maybe not, the Redcap had some very different ideas. He refused to lend his jeep to Moore, who called on his vast knowledge of the English language and his boyish charm to persuade the reluctant MP into swapping his jeep for the motorcycle. Once behind the wheel of his newly acquired vehicle he bade a swift farewell to a disgruntled policeman.

But matters got even worse when he found a supply dump. No one offered him any help whatsoever but stood and watched as he loaded boxes of ammunition onto the jeep. News obviously travelled much faster than ammunition because, on his return to the Squadron, he was told that he was in trouble with the Provost staff. He was amazed to discover that they wanted to place him under immediate close arrest for the theft of Army property, namely the jeep. However, the threat was withdrawn and Terry Moore was told not to do it again.

Bob Lowson had suffered similar treatment when he had been sent into Termoli to find more mortar rounds.

There was an air of desertion about the place but after a hurried search I at last managed to find a Sergeant Major who I hoped could supply me with what was urgently needed. Instead of receiving any form of help I found myself being smiled at and asked a silly question. 'Do you really have the men to use these?' My reply to him was fairly curt and to the point, 'Of course I've got the men; now just give me the rounds.'

Major Harry Poat, regarded as a true gentleman through-out the Squadron, also made his feelings clear when he came across a senior officer from 78th Division.

> You should know that we are terribly disappointed with the support that we didn't receive from you and rather than wearing battleaxes as your shoulder flashes it would possibly be more appropriate if you had them changed for crossed knitting needles.

In his frustration, Poat was unaware that 78th Division's units were suffering the same stringencies as his own.

At 7.00 a.m. Lance-Sergeant Goldsmith, or 'Buttercup Joe' as he was better known to the men, was ordered to move out and make his way through the railway station to the goods yard. It was hoped that once in his new position he might hold an important section of the line. Goldsmith made a quick assessment of the surrounding area as soon as he arrived and chose what he regarded as the best vantage point. He paid scant regard to the fact that he had decided to position himself atop a large storage tank containing some 500 gallons of fuel oil, or that he was a one match a day chain smoker. In his opinion the main reason for his choice was that its extra height gave him the best field of fire. Nor did it seem to bother him that once spotted he would be a very easy target for enemy gunners. Throughout the day he was subjected to heavy fire but he had made his decision and he held his nerve along with his position. Goldsmith would not be moved. Doggedly he remained on his vantage point.

At 10.00 a.m. Lance-Sergeant Chalky White, com-manding a sub-section during one of the many German counter-attacks, was finding it increasingly difficult to hold his position. He saw that the enemy were pushing extremely hard towards his area of the line; his men were coming under intensive mortar and small arms fire with the weight and strength of that fire increasing to very dangerous levels. Chalky was beginning to think that his small section were being left with no choice other than to pull back and surrender some vital ground. But shortly after making the move he realised that he might have made a dangerous mistake since his change of position could allow the Germans to advance even further and force the raiders into yielding yet more ground.

White decided that as the man responsible for the error he would have to try to rectify it and, ordering his men to remain where they were and give him covering fire, he tried to make his way back to their original position. The Germans spotted his move instantly and threw everything they had at him to try to dislodge him once again. Round after round plunged into the area and shells exploded all around him. But he would not be moved and despite the severity of the fire he held the ground he had retaken and fought off the Germans for another two hours. Once he felt that the threat to his position had receded he decided to move once again, took charge of another section and led it throughout the rest of the day. During the same fierce enemy counter-attack on the line to the west of Termoli C Section was also under extreme pressure.

C Section suffered a very severe blow when several of its men were wounded and their section commander, Captain Sandy Wilson, and Lance-Corporal Scherzinger were killed. They had been manning an anti-tank gun when a heavy salvo of mortars straddled their position. The gun had been placed behind a large haystack for cover but the

German fire set the stack alight and it was burning fiercely as it collapsed suddenly, trapping both men. The only member of the section not to be wounded in this bombardment was Lance-Corporal Duncan McLennon. He showed total disregard for the fact that he was still under very heavy fire and put himself into even greater danger by carrying, dragging or pushing his wounded comrades back to an aid post.

But that act of courage was not enough for McLennon. He then returned to his original position near the burning haystack, picked up a discarded Bren gun and started laying down heavy and accurate fire. His bravery was instrumental in holding up the advancing Germans during the rest of the fighting. He was eventually joined by a section from No.40 Commando, through whom he managed to get a message back to his headquarters telling them of his position.

Under the superb leadership of Alex Muirhead, the men of the mortar sections had the last word in what had been an intense and dangerous battle at about 3 o'clock that afternoon. They finally silenced the enemy and allowed the Squadron's tenuous position to be held. It was only fitting that the men from the mortar sections were involved at the finish of the campaign as they had fired the Squadron's first shots in anger at Capo-Murro-di-Porco.

By now the units of 78th Division were on the offensive and the raiders were able to witness a classic attack by infantry with excellent armour support. This attack was carried out in two phases by the Irish Brigade who had landed, under fire, during the night and then moved into the perimeter to strengthen the line. In the first phase of the Irish Brigade attack 6th Royal Inniskilling Fusiliers and 1st Royal Irish Fusiliers had advanced and taken the ridge with the aid of fifteen Shermans of the *Trois Rivières* Regiment and the fire support of a field artillery bombardment. The Irish Fusiliers led the way – their Gaelic motto, *Faugh A Ballagh!*, literally means 'clear the way!' – to take the brickworks where Major Anderson VC of the Argylls had fallen, and then on to the ridge. On the left flank the Inniskillings fought through close woodland and open fields to reach and take their objective. By 5.00 p.m. the ridge was secure in the hands of the Irish Brigade and the Canadian tankies. Major Bala Bredin, second-in-command of the Irish Fusiliers, commented that the Canadians were very enthusiastic and fully lived up to their motto of 'Have a go, Joe'; this may have been because it was their first taste of action. Later in the afternoon the brigade's third battalion, 2nd London Irish Rifles, who had held the brigade base line as the fusilier battalions advanced, moved up from the goods yard along the coast road and, overcoming resistance around the cemetery, were on the Sinacre river by nightfall thus anchoring the extreme right of the British bridgehead.

As the Rifles advanced the Raiding Squadron added its contribution to the covering fire with their machine guns and mortars. Mayne had been thoroughly delighted to learn of the arrival of the Irish Brigade and for the first time in many days there was a grin on his face. He turned proudly to his men and told them: 'You'll be all right now lads, the Irish are coming and they'll sort it all out for us.' But he had no way of knowing that some of the Rifles had already sorted out his kit for him. Much to his disgust, he later discovered what had happened to his belongings. Luckily for the person, or persons, involved he never did find out who was responsible.

With the battle for Termoli over the remaining men of the Special Service Brigade were relieved. At last light on 6 October the Special Raiding Squadron and No.40 (Royal Marine) Commando[1] marched back towards the harbour and that same evening No.3 Commando embarked at 7.45 bound for Bari. Together they had played their part in stopping the advance of 16th Panzer Division and had demonstrated the same determination in a defensive action as they had so often done in offence. However, many felt that they had fought a very lonely battle and some even considered that they had been denied the support they ought to have had. But loneliness is a major part of the infantryman's life in a defensive battle and the circumstances prevailing around Termoli, especially with the very heavy rain bogging down the advance of 78th Division, meant that the support provided for all those in the bridgehead fell short of what had been planned. Even the Irish Brigade attack should have had additional armoured support but these latter tanks had been held up by an anti-tank obstacle and the assault had to be made with only the *Trois Rivières'* squadron. Bridging equipment was also in short supply as Eighth Army tried to maintain two corps-strength advances and the army's long logistical tail. During the battle for Termoli many of the experiences of Mayne and his men had been traumatic and at times the consequences had been tragic. Despite what some outside the Squadron thought of them, they were a highly disciplined unit, did everything together and always knew what to expect from each other. That was why they felt more comfortable relying on their own skills.

From the first landing at Capo-Murro-di-Porco until the Squadron was relieved after the Termoli battle, the

dominating figure of Major Robert Blair Mayne DSO
had been highly visible during every action. Much to the
consternation of his men he constantly indulged himself
in his passion for photography which he often practised
while walking about in full view of the enemy. On other
occasions he was constantly involved in action. When
not fighting alongside his own men he could be spotted
going among the troops of any other units who happened
to be in his area. When he came across them he would
offer whatever help he thought might be helpful. Paddy
Mayne was a born leader who had long mastered the art
of getting the best out of his men. At times he would
achieve great results by a piece of forceful cajoling, while
at others all that it required would be a few simple words
of encouragement.

Wounded in action between 3 and 6 October 1943 were
Major Fraser MC, Captain Melot MC, Corporals Allen,
Kerr and Sturmey; Lance-Corporals Frizzle, Gilmour,
Kenna, McLennon, Mullan and Rennie; Privates Oldcroft,
Bowen, Burgess, Canning, Cave, Fergusson, McLachlan,
Mylor, Halifax, Vango, Knight, Monteith, Blair, Bond,
O'Gorman and Singer.

As a result of the Termoli battle a number of gallantry
awards were made to the Squadron: Captain Marsh was
awarded the DSO while Staff-Sergeant Clark, Sergeant
Campbell, Lance-Sergeants White and Goldsmith, Lance-
Corporals Moore, Ridler and McLennon and Private
Ralphs were each awarded the Military Medal.

The battle at Termoli was to be the end of the fighting
in Italy for this small unit, which had paid a very heavy
price for its successes. At the outset of operations, some
four months earlier, the Special Raiding Squadron had

deployed a total strength of 280 men. Some had been returned to their parent units for disciplinary reasons or transferred to other units but many more had been put out of action due to wounds received in battle. Moreover, as the survivors fought on into Italy, they met much stiffer opposition from highly trained and experienced German soldiers. Their casualty totals were thirty killed in action, fifty-four wounded and twenty-two taken prisoner. The other two units of the SS Brigade also suffered. No.3 Commando had five men killed and twenty-nine wounded, No.40 Commando suffered six killed and thirty wounded while 2nd SAS had one killed and two wounded.

Operation DEVON was an outstanding success. After taking the enemy completely by surprise, the SS Brigade and 78th Division had to fight back with tenacity to hold Termoli. Though hard pressed on several occasions, their doggedness and determined resistance frustrated every effort of a superior force to inflict not only defeat but annihilation. Within a few hours of their landing, the SS Brigade alone killed more than 150 enemy. Almost the same number, including forty wounded, were taken prisoner. The Termoli landing not only gave Eighth Army a valuable harbour but, by outflanking the left flank of the enemy's line, denied him the important Naples–Campobasso–Termoli lateral road. It hastened considerably the speed of his retirement and caused the German command to revise its plan to check the Allied advance.

Over the following three days, the Squadron returned to Termoli to rest. Many bottles of wine were consumed but the overall mood was downbeat and morose. Terry Moore summed up their feelings:

When you took the first drink it was in relief that you had survived, the second was that you would be able to take part in the next action and the third would be for your fallen comrades who had not been so lucky.

Sid Payne had to take part in what was probably the hardest and most sombre of jobs. He was one of the five-man burial detail. Due to the intensity of the battle, the remains of the dead had lain in the monastery for two days. Several had been blown apart and what little remained of them was virtually unrecognisable. As he helped place the remains of his dead comrades in their shallow graves in the monastery grounds, he could not help remembering the earlier conversation he had had with young Titch Davison on board the landing craft just before they had landed at Termoli.

A number of men spent some time visiting their wounded comrades to try to cheer them up. Even though there was an obvious feeling of gloom hanging over everyone, some retained their sharp wit and found time for the usual round of banter. Douglas Monteith was informed that he was to be court-martialled for trying to interfere with the nuns. He was to be charged with trying to gain entry into the monastery by using his head to break through the brick walls.

One incident that did shed a little ray of light on their day was the return of Lieutenant John Tonkin to their ranks. He had managed to give his captors the slip and make good his escape. On 10 October Lieutenant-General Dempsey, commanding XIII Corps, spoke to the assembled Squadron.

It is just three months since we landed in Sicily and during that time you have carried out four successful operations. You were originally only lent to me for the first operation, that of Capo-Murro-di-Porco. That was a brilliant operation, brilliantly planned and brilliantly carried out. Your orders were to capture and destroy a coastal battery, but you did more. I left it entirely up to you what you did after that and you went on to capture two more batteries and a very large number of prisoners, an excellent piece of work. No one then could have foretold that things would have turned out as they have. You were to have returned to the Middle East after that operation but you then went on to take Augusta. You had no time for careful planning, but still you were highly successful. Then came Bagnara and finally Termoli, the landing at Termoli completely upset the Germans' schedule and the balance of their forces by introducing a threat to the north of Rome. They were obliged to bring to the East coast the 16th Panzer Division that was in reserve in the Naples area. They had orders, which have since come into our hands, to recapture Termoli at all costs and drive the British into the sea. These orders, thanks to you, they were unable to carry out. It had another effect though, it eased the pressure on the American Fifth Army and as you have probably heard they are now advancing. When I first saw you at Az-zib and told you that you were going to work with 13 Corps, I was very impressed by you and everything that I saw. When I told you that you had a coastal battery to destroy I was convinced that it was the right sort of job for you. In all my Military career and in my time I have commanded many units but I have never met a unit in which I had such confidence as I have in yours, and I mean that.

Dempsey obviously knew and understood the calibre of the men who stood in front of him. As he was taking his leave he expressed his deep regret and said: 'I hope that the association may be renewed at a later date.'

General Montgomery also paid the Squadron a brief visit and told its members that he hoped to be going back to England soon and although he was making no promises he said that wherever he went he would like the men of the Special Air Service Regiment to be with him. His short speech to the assembled soldiers bore great similarity to one he had recently used when speaking to members of a Canadian regiment who were also under his command.

On 12 October the Squadron once again boarded a landing craft, No.179, which took them some 175 miles down the coast to Molfetta. The journey was peaceful and on arrival they disembarked and moved into billets. The raiders were glad to remain totally static for the rest of the month and enjoy some well earned rest and recuperation. By then it had been decided that there was no further role for the Squadron in the region and its soldiers boarded a destroyer for the trip to Bari on the first leg of the journey that would take them back to Britain.

During their short time on board the destroyer the raiders began bartering with the crew over some of the souvenirs they had brought aboard. The money raised from these transactions was to be used for the families of those killed in action. One rather large American cook had taken a shine to a German Luger and decided that he would take it from its new owner, Private Casey, or 'Killer' as he was known in the Squadron. The cook soon discovered how serious a mistake he had made. One large right hook was all that was required and the rather foolish American took his leave of the ship, plummeting into the water over the guardrail. After witnessing his fate, the other sailors were only too glad to see reason and eagerly made deals with the rest of the would-be entrepreneurs. Terry Moore was among those looking on in almost total disbelief: 'The poor American never really stood a chance. Casey was very well known as being a hard hitter and the punch seemed to come from somewhere around his ankles.'

At Bari the Squadron embarked on an American-built LST (Landing Ship, Tank) to cross a very rough Mediterranean to North Africa. The next port of call for the now seasoned travellers was to be Philippeville in Algeria but the majority had a terrible journey and suffered very badly from seasickness. It was David Danger's turn to be on cooking duties: 'I don't think that I will ever be able to forget the look on some of their faces when I served them up the standard Army breakfast of fried bacon and baked beans.' They were again in the company of their comrades from 2nd SAS at Philippeville and together they journeyed by train to Algiers all feeling very happy because, if everything went to plan, they were on their way home. Opportunities to exchange views with local residents were never to be missed and so during the journey they bartered and made numerous deals with the many Arabs they encountered. They may also have invented a term commonly used today, 'meals on wheels', as they had to prepare and eat all their own meals while on the move.

All that took place in the none too salubrious boxcars provided for their transport. It was a very long way from the comfort and style to which they had become accustomed on *Ulster Monarch*.

Conditions failed to improve when they reached Algiers and they spent a very uncomfortable Christmas holiday. Food was not a problem – they gorged themselves by eating huge quantities of oranges – but they suffered very badly after being bitten by some rather large and hungry mosquitoes that must have seen them as a new source of a good meal. That uncomfortable episode was due to their camp being situated in a forest overlooking the harbour. Thankfully, their stay was short and the final leg of the homeward journey started on Boxing Day as they embarked on a troopship and set sail for Glasgow.

The Squadron, its soldiers now back on British soil, was given some very welcome leave before moving into a new training base around the Lanfine Estate near Darvel in Ayrshire. For everyone concerned it was to be a very happy reunion with their inspirational leader Paddy Mayne. He had gained some very valuable experience about the tactics required during beach landings and had flown home much earlier to begin planning for the next phase of the war. The Special Raiding Squadron title, under which they had fought so bravely, was discontinued and they reverted to their former title of 1st Special Air Service Regiment.

Second SAS had also arrived 'home' from North Africa and the two Regiments were joined by two newly-formed French battalions and a Belgian squadron, providing very rapid growth to brigade strength. As the SAS was to become part of the airborne forces it was decided to change to the wearing of the red beret. Mayne, as usual, had his own thoughts and refused to conform by continuing to wear his original sand-coloured one. But now the 'old hands' would take over and begin training the many new recruits and volunteers who would be added for the forthcoming assaults on Nazi-occupied mainland Europe. With such a large increase in numbers it was important to Paddy Mayne that he had the assistance of his experienced officers, senior ranks and troopers. Corporal David Danger had been selected for officer training but he could not refuse the personal request from Mayne to stay and help with the new intakes. As he was an extremely good signaller he had been given a vital task to perform on his commanding officer's jeep. His orders were to construct and install a public address system on the vehicle for the playing of music. 'You can imagine the strange looks we used to get from the locals as we drove along the narrow streets and lanes in convoy while playing Count John McCormack and Percy French records.'

Once again, events would necessitate change in their role and tactics as they would revert to the more mobile, specialised warfare perfected in the desert rather than the brute force used in the Mediterranean. The Regiment would be reunited with what were, perhaps, their two favourite pieces of equipment, the jeep and the twin Vickers machine gun. While the basic layout of the vehicle would be the same, their new operational areas would require a large increase in armoured protection. The fighting would be very difficult and costly as they fought their way through Europe but the bravery and skill displayed by the jeep squadrons would be so great that Canadian tank crews affectionately referred to them as 'our little friends in the mechanised mess tins'. The newly promoted Lieutenant-Colonel Robert Blair Mayne DSO and Bar was given command of 1st Special Air Service Regiment and would lead them through even stiffer tests and battles.

Note

1. The effect of the action at Termoli and the pride felt by No.40 RM Commando means that 3 October is marked annually as Termoli Day.

Appendices

Appendix I

The War Record of a Glorious Monarch

Ulster Monarch was the ship used by the Special Raiding Squadron as a mother ship but the vessel had an illustrious career all of her own. Built in 1929 and with a gross weight of 3,791 tons, *Monarch* could steam at 17 knots. She was owned by the Ulster Imperial Line with which she served as a ferry on the Belfast–Liverpool route before being requisitioned by the Admiralty in 1939. As a troopship, still flying the Red Ensign, *Ulster Monarch* first saw action on 7 September 1939 when she carried troops of the British Expeditionary Force to France. She was commissioned under the White Ensign in October 1940 and, until 1942, operated as a troopship, at first between Iceland and the Clyde and then along the West African coast.

Recalled from these duties, *Monarch* left Freetown, unescorted, and headed once again for the Clyde to be converted into an LSI (H), (Landing Ship Infantry (Hand)). Such ships carried six Landing Craft Assault (LCAs), which were carried under hand-operated radial davits or projecting spurs, hence the (H) in the designation. In her new role, *Monarch* could carry 580 troops – she had the highest capacity of the ten LSIs (H) that were commissioned into the Royal Navy – and was also fitted with a 12-pounder gun as well as a complement of anti-aircraft weapons. On her journey back to Scotland the seas became very rough and her engines developed some problems that made manoeuvring difficult. The heavy seas also caused electrical troubles, putting out all the lights on the boat decks but these troubles were soon rectified and, after ten days, the ship docked at Greenock. The re-fit came too late for *Monarch* to be used in Operation JUBILEE, the Dieppe raid, in August 1942 and so her first assignment in her new role was during Operation TORCH later that year, landing American Rangers at Aruze, east of Oran in Algeria, where she was one of the first ships to dock with reinforcements and supplies.

Having dropped the Rangers at Oran, *Ulster Monarch* set sail the following morning accompanied by *Royal Scotsman*, another LSI (H), and both went to the assistance of the Canadian Pacific liner *Duchess of Bedford* which had run aground in heavy seas. The two LCIs managed to save the liner. *Monarch* then returned to Oran and picked up the survivors from two American Coastguard cutters, *Wainey* and *Hartland,* which had crashed the boom under heavy enemy fire. Next, *Monarch* sailed for Britain as part of a convoy that had to run the gauntlet of German U-boats lying in wait in the Straits of Gibraltar. The escort carrier HMS *Avenger* and two transport ships were sunk on this trip.

After another re-fit *Monarch* joined what Lord Mountbatten had described as 'the spearhead of the invasion of Sicily fleet' in which she would take part in the actions described in this book. After that she continued to carry troops and stores from Sicily to Tripoli and other North African ports and it was during her last voyage to Tripoli that she had her worst wartime experience. On the night of Thursday 19 August 1943 *Monarch* was in convoy with three other ships, and steaming ahead at 15½ knots in slight seas and fine weather, when they were spotted and attacked by a single enemy aircraft that made a low-level bombing and strafing attack. Three bombs were dropped from a height of 800 feet, two of which were near misses. However, the third struck her on the port quarter, destroying the mounting for the ship's 12-pounder gun, while the poop deck and shell plating were also pierced. This was where the fuel and ammunition was stored; the bomb penetrated the deck and exited the hull just above the water line. The fuel was set alight and it was only the skill of the crew that prevented a magazine explosion that would have destroyed *Ulster Monarch*. Lieutenant-Commander T.F. Wrigley was commended for the bravery he had shown during this action. Fortunately, the damage inflicted on her was not too severe but, sadly, three men were killed and five were seriously wounded. *Monarch* was able to continue in the convoy and reached Tripoli where repairs were carried out and the dead and wounded taken off. Two weeks later *Monarch* was back in action, this time landing the first assault wave of troops at Salerno. After this she continued operating in the Mediterranean before returning to the United Kingdom for further repairs.

On D-Day, 6 June 1944, *Ulster Monarch* lay with the first assault forces off Courseulles, where again the weather was bad as she landed her two flights of Canadian and Scottish troops. On this occasion one of her LCAs failed to return and another was damaged badly when it hit a mine, although only one man was lost. After the initial assaults of D-Day, *Monarch* made a further eighty-three trips, either from Plymouth or Portsmouth, across the Channel in a shuttle service. During this period she carried many senior naval and military passengers and delivered some 5,512 bags of mail and 1,000 tons of urgent stores to the beaches and Port Winston, the Mulberry harbour at Arromanches. In October 1944 she was assigned to general shuttle duties that consisted of carrying troops from Southampton to Le Havre, Cherbourg, Ostend and other destinations. Between the D-Day landings and VE day, *Ulster Monarch* carried a total of 36,946 personnel on round trips.

After the war she returned to her original role as a ferry between Belfast and Liverpool and continued in this role until 1964 when her owners, by then P&O, took her out of service and had her scrapped. So ended a glorious career, but her memory lives on as the surviving members of the Special Raiding Squadron still remember her fondly.

Appendix II

The Men and Leadership of the Squadron

The four seaborne landings at Capo-Murro-di-Porco, Augusta, Bagnara and Termoli and the subsequent actions could have been likened to four miniature D-Day landings. They were planned to be the beginning of the invasion of mainland Europe and the part played by the Special Raiding Squadron was significant in each. These operations were carried out under varying degrees of difficulty: foul weather caused havoc with the initial landing and as the Squadron pushed farther inland communications and, in some cases, lack of support from other units did not help. At times, due to the unpredictable nature of war, there was very little advance warning about the next operation and planning played an important part in the thinking of Paddy Mayne. His meticulous attention to detail was always very evident to his men and they recall how, on leaving any of his briefings, no one of whatever rank was ever left in any doubt about his role in the greater plan. Every single detail of the operation was covered, where, when, how and why. This had always been Mayne's way, right from the early days of his rugby career at Ards RFC; there his planning and leadership qualities were spotted very early on and were instrumental in the choice of Paddy Mayne for club captain.

What must also not be forgotten is the immense quality and skills of the men who fought under his command. They were themselves well educated, highly capable and very brave young men. Many were seasoned veterans, professional soldiers who had seen active service along with Mayne in the early commando units and again in the Middle East campaigns with the Special Air Service. They were handpicked soldiers and had shown themselves to be a match for anyone. Operation HUSKY was a major offensive, the first planned invasion of Europe and a joint operation between American and British forces which had been discussed by Roosevelt and Churchill at the Casablanca conference in January 1943. Both leaders felt that the capture of Sicily would be vital for the safety of the Mediterranean and would tie down large numbers of the German and Italian forces in that region. To be used as 'shock troops' was relatively new ground for the Special Raiding Squadron and some felt that this was a role that they should never have been asked to undertake. It is also quite possible that there may have been a school of thought that saw them as expendable. Whichever of these is true would be pure speculation, but the facts and figures speak for themselves. From day one the SRS carried out their tasks and many more with great courage and determination as the many decorations awarded to them show. The success of the men on the ground proved yet again that the Special Air Service could, and did, adapt to any role it was asked to undertake.

Appendix III

Nominal Roll

Name	Rank	Army No.	Parent Unit	Notes
Adamson, E	Cpl	2938313	Camerons	
Adamson, E Y	Pte	4399392	E. Yorks	
Ainsley, G	L/Cpl			PW, Termoli
Alcock, R	L/Cpl	5950912	Beds & Herts	
Aldcroft, W	L/Cpl			
Allan, J	Pte			WIA, Capo-Murro.
Allan, W W	Cpl	2031580	RAMC	PW, Termoli
Ancona, J	Tpr	5885138	Recce	WIA, Augusta
Anderson, J	L/Cpl			RTU, 16 Aug
Arbuckle, J F S	Pte	2985863	A&S Hldrs	
Archer, D	Sgt	130927	RASC	
Arnold, W	L/Bdr	889850	RA	
Ashton, S	Pte	2182036	RWK	
Ashurst, E	Gnr	1533486	RA	
Asquith, J	L/Cpl			PW , Termoli

Name	Rank	Army No.	Parent Unit	Notes
Austen, E P	Cpl	214964	RASC	
Badger, E	Sgt			WIA, Bagnara
Baggott, A	Pte	5732872	BW	
Baker, A	L/Cpl	2615255	G. Gds	
Ball, J H	Pte	5186123	RA	KIA, Bagnara
Bamsey, S	Pte	6013473	Essex	
Barnby, D G	Capt	176046	E. Yorks	Adj 8 Aug '43
Bass, G R	Pte	5338640	Queen's	
Bateman, K	L/Cpl	5572359	Wilts	
Beech, T	Gdsm	2720087	Ir. Gds	
Bell, D E	L/Cpl	7626887	RAOC	
Belsham, F	Cpl	6012851	Essex	
Bennett, R	Sgt	2617533	G. Gds	
Bentley, J W	Cpl	7521867	RAMC	KIA, Augusta
Bercott	Lt			
Blair, V	Pte			WIA, Termoli
Blanche, S	Gdsm	2657391	Coldm Gds	
Bowen, J S	Gnr	899930	RA	WIA, Termoli
Bowles, F	Pte	70453	ACC	
Bowman, J	Spr	1879074	RE	
Broadleday, J	L/Cpl	192637	RASC	
Bromfield, J H	Tpr	410663	CLY	
Brook, H	L/Cpl	2615070	G. Gds	
Brophy, M J	Pte	6353031	RWK	RFHQ 21 Sep
Brough, W G	S/Sgt	2695138	S. Gds	
Brundle, I	L/Cpl			PW, Termoli
Bryson, W	L/Cpl	2880083	RAVC	WIA, Bagnara
Buchanan, A	Pte			RTU, 8 Sep
Buckley, J	Pte	7389040	RAMC	PW, Termoli

Name	Rank	Army No.	Parent Unit	Notes
Bunfield, N	Sgt			
Burgess, H	Gnr	889974	RHA	WIA, Termoli
Burgess, W	Tpr	4205908	RAC	
Burn, H	Pte			RTU, 16 Aug
Butler, J	Sgt	4266826	ACC	
Cademy, A	Gdsm	2656472	Coldm Gds	
Campbell, M M	Sgt	2982964	A&S Hldrs	
Canning, B	Pte			WIA, Termoli
Casey, F	Pte	6309236	R. Sussex	
Cassidy, G	Pte	6028881	RWK	KIA, Termoli
Caton, G.	Cpl	1455205	RA	KIA, Capo-Murro
Cattell, C	Sgt	6141548	E. Surreys	
Cave, J	Gnr	1515888	RA	WIA, Termoli
Chappell, C	Cpl	1887939	RE	
Chick, R	Cpl	7895914		
Clark, J A	S/Sgt	80666	RASC	
Clarke, F C	Spr	7014058	RE	WIA, Bagnara
Cleverley, C	L/Cpl	324485	ACC	
Collier, W	Tpr	7902951	RAC	
Collison, G	Pte	14215003	RWK	
Commerie	Pte			PW, Termoli
Conley, S	Spr	2068148	RE	
Corbett, F	Spr	1876396	RE	
Corbett, J H	Gnr	846834	RA	
Cordiner, R	L/Cpl			PW, Termoli
Corps, T	Bdr	861127	RA	
Costello, R	L/Cpl	2018084	RE	WIA, Capo-Murro
Cranford, H H	SQMS	146408	RASC	

Name	Rank	Army No.	Parent Unit	Notes
Crawford, J	L/Cpl	494713	RA	
Crisp, L	L/Cpl	884074	RA	KIA, Termoli
Cummings, L	L/Cpl			PW, Termoli
Cunningham, J	Cpl	6400007	R. Sussex	
Dalziel, C	L/Sgt	874261	S. Gds	
Danger, D L P	Sgn	2598982	R. Sigs	
Davidson, A	L/Cpl	2886121	Gordons	
Davis, P J G	Lt	184425	Queen's	
Davison, S	Pte	4627437	DLI	KIA, Termoli
Dawson, J	Pte	2992436	A&S Hldrs	
Deakins, W A	Sgt	1886410	RE	
Docherty, J	Pte	2985655	A&S Hldrs	
Downes, G	L/Sgt	2695796	S. Gds	
Draper, W	L/Cpl	7610041	RAOC	
Dray, A E	Pte	5623862	Devon	
Duffy, W P	L/Cpl			PW, Termoli
Duke, S	Pte	791868	ACC	
Dunbar, J	Tpr	7955707	RAC	
Duncan, A	Pte	2759014	BW	KIA, Termoli
Duncanson, G	Pte	3184679	KOSB	
DuVivier, J	Sgt	2885910	Gordons	
Earle, E	Tpr	7959279	RAC	
Eccles, D	L/Sgt	2735399	W. Gds	WIA, Augusta
Eccles, W	Pte	3319331	HLI	
Ewing, D	L/Cpl	3059224	S. Gds	
Fairbrother, W	Pte	138614	ACC	
Fassam, J W	L/Cpl	874242	RA	KIA, Termoli
Fenton, J	L/Cpl			SOS 15 Sep
Ferguson, C	Dvr	135738	RASC	

Name	Rank	Army No.	Parent Unit	Notes
Fergusson, D	Pte	3311851	HLI	WIA, Termoli
Finlay, J S	Sgt	1436147	RA	KIA, Termoli
Finnimore, W	Pte	3959698	Welch	PW, Termoli
Fitch, E K	Gnr	897428	RA	
Flower, J	Dvr	61851	RASC	
Flynn, M	Pte	5346037	R. Berks	
Frame, A	L/Sgt	3246893	Cameronians	WIA, Augusta
Francis, E L W	Capt	150524		Admin Officer, G List
Fraser, W	Major	132513	Gordons	WIA, Termoli
Frizzle	L/Cpl			WIA, Termoli
Gallier, R	L/Bdr	1465403	RA	
Gardner, A	Pte	2762989	BW	
Gibb, D	Tpr	7952596	RAC	
Gilmour, G	L/Cpl			WIA, Termoli
Glacken, J	Pte	3325345	HLI	WIA, Bagnara
Gladwell, R	L/Cpl			
Glaze, D	WO II (CSM)	551100	APTC	
Goldie, B	Cpl	3185949	S. Gds	
Goldsmith, R	Sgt	6397316	R. Sussex	
Gordon, J	L/Cpl	420622	L&B Yeo	
Govan, J C W	L/Cpl	3057065	RASC	
Grant, C	L/Cpl			KIA, Termoli
Griffiths, E	Pte	6001263	Essex	PW, Termoli
Grimster, E	Pte	3661499	Gordons	WIA, Bagnara/ KIA, Termoli
Guard, R	Pte	2929492	L'pl Scots	
Gunn, P M	Capt	128655	RAMC	

Name	Rank	Army No.	Parent Unit	Notes
Gurmin, M H	Lt			SOS Palestine 8 Aug
Hair, J	Pte	2763568	BW	
Halifax, W	Pte	2828953	Seaforth	WIA, Termoli
Hall, J	L/Bdr	900883	RA	WIA, Augusta
Hall, J	Tpr	4388619	Yorks Hsrs	
Hancock				
Harding, J H	Lt		Sigs Officer	RFHQ Palestine 20 July
Harris, H	L/Cpl	6970161	RB	
Harrison, D I	Capt	145763	Cheshire	
Harrison, S	Pte	6407758	R. Sussex	
Hay, A	Pte	3249963	Cameronians	
Hazell, E	Tpr	863029	3 King's Own Hsrs	
Hearn, W H	Pte	5625251	Devon	KIA, Termoli
Heavens, R E	Sgt	820065	RHA	
Hemsworth, C A	Pte	4398964	E. Yorks	
Henderson, J B	Sgt	2695776	S. Gds	KIA, Termoli
Higgins, T	L/Cpl	3523095	Recce	
Higham, R	L/Cpl	3711552	KORR	
Hill, H	Pte	6298443	Buffs	WIA, Murro-De-Porco
Hill, J	Fus	6479803	RF	WIA, Bagnara
Hine, A	Dvr	6442020	RASC	
Hodgkinson, L	L/Cpl	843285	RA	KIA, Termoli
Holmes, J A	Cpl	328084	RAC	
Howell, W K	Sgn	6348757	RWK	KIA, Bagnara
Hugman, H	Spr	5827088	RE	

Name	Rank	Army No.	Parent Unit	Notes
Hutchinson, G	L/Bdr	908535	RA	Posted 3 Commando
Irvine, D	Pte	2934338	Camerons	
Jackson, R W	Pte	4399418	E. Yorks	
James, D	Fus	4192780	RNF	
Jessiman, J R	Bdr	1468628	RA	
Johnstone, E	Cpl	3424119	Cameronians	
Jones, T	L/Cpl	2989384	A&S Hldrs	
Jones, W	Gnr	1482674	RA	
Jones, W S E	Bdr	1428802	RA	
Josling, F W	Gnr	974097	RA	
Judge	Pte			PW, Termoli
Kenna	L/Cpl			WIA, Termoli
Kennedy, W F B	Cpl	320025	R. Scots Greys	
Kerr, H	Cpl			WIA, Termoli
Kershaw, D	WO II (CSM)	4121633	G. Gds	
Kirk	Pte			WIA, Bagnara
Kilroy, W	Gnr	1526035	RA	
Kingsbury,	L/Cpl			RFHQ 10 Sep
Kinnivane, J	L/Cpl	6094156	Queen's	
Knight	Pte			WIA, Termoli
Lake, D	Pte	1610622	ACC	
Langfield, D	Pte	4196640	RWK	
Lansley, L	Sgn	5835133	R. Sigs	
Latham, A	Gnr	872961	RA	
Law, A	Dvr	132614	RASC	
Law, G D	Tpr	3603627	RAC	
Lawrence, R	Gnr	5181379	RA	

Name	Rank	Army No.	Parent Unit	Notes
Lea, R V	Major			SOS Palestine 8 Aug
Lea	Pte			PW, Termoli
Leadbetter, W	Bdr	921086	RA	
Leitch, J	Cpl	2698540	S. Gds	
Lepine, E	Capt	182207	S. Staffs	
Lilley, E T	S/Sgt	2660913	Coldm Gds	
Little, J T	L/Cpl	2938050	Camerons	WIA, Bagnara
Logan	Pte			
Lowson, R	Cpl	2929977	L'pl Scots	WIA, Termoli
Lunt, R G	Capt	14434	RAChD	To SS Bde 31 July
MacLennon, D M	L/Sgt	2929317	Recce	
McAlpin, W M	Pte	3058778	Gordons	KIA, Termoli
McBeath	Pte			PW, Termoli
McDiarmid, J	L/Sgt	7263971	BW	WIA, Bagnara
McDonald, J	L/Cpl	4128862	RNF	KIA, Termoli
McDonald	Pte			PW, Termoli
McDougall, R E	Spr	2079913	RE	
McEvoy, C	Sgt			PW, Termoli
McFarlane, C	Dvr	215922	RASC	
McGee, E	Pte	7304702	RAMC	
McGinn, C	Cpl	2888389	Gordons	
McGrath, A	Pte	6014932	Essex	
McKenzie, J	Pte	7264124	Camerons	PW, Termoli
McLaughlan, B T	Pte	2888636	Gordons	KIA, Termoli
McLelland, J	Cfn	7609282	REME	WIA, Termoli
McLeod, A	Pte	2822451	Seaforth	

Name	Rank	Army No.	Parent Unit	Notes
McNinch, W M	Sgt	322865	RAC	KIA, Termoli
McSwiggan, D	L/Cpl	2880632	Gordons	
Markham, J	Sgt			PW, Termoli
Marrs, P	Sgt	7357255	RAMC	
Marsh, J A	Capt	109524	DCLI	
Marshall, G	L/Cpl	5953115	Beds & Herts	
Martin, R	Pte	3837105	DLI	
Maskell, H	Pte	5440904		PW, Termoli
Masker	Pte			PW, Termoli
Mayne, R B	Major	87306	RUR	
Melot, R M E	Capt	163579		Int Officer; WIA, Termoli
Midgely	L/Cpl			WIA, Bagnara
Miller, R	L/Bdr	1578003	RA	
Mitchell, A	Cpl			WIA, Bagnara
Monks, L	L/Cpl	7899682	RAC	
Monteith, D	Pte	5621690	Devon	WIA, Termoli
Moore, T V	L/Cpl	4539369	RA	
Morgan, R	Pte	3726765	Dorset	
Morris, H	Lt	75895	UDF (1 Pretoria Hldrs)	
Morris, J	Fus	4204478	RWF	
Morrison, A	Gnr	1774643	RA	
Moss, D	Tpr	6405636	RAC	
Muirhead, A D	Capt	134303	Worcester	
Mullan, H	L/Cpl	2935098	Camerons	WIA, Termoli
Munro, N	Pte	3325330	HLI	
Musk, E	L/Cpl	5830939	Cambs	

Name	Rank	Army No.	Parent Unit	Notes
Myler	Pte			WIA, Termoli
Neary, A	Gnr	914042	RA	
Nicholson, J	Pte	2930645	Camerons	
Nixon, J	Pte	3189432	KOSB	
Noble, J	L/Cpl	321442	RASC	
O'Dowd, C	Sgt	2719054	Ir. Gds	KIA, Termoli
O'Gorman, B M	Dvr	221813	RASC	WIA, Termoli
Oldcroft	Pte			WIA, Termoli
O'Neill, J	Pte	150310	ACC	
O'Neill, J	Pte	7014295	BW	
Orr, D	Tpr	ME/7950016	RAC	
Overend, E	Rfn	3711341	KORR	
Oxley, R	L/Sgt	2989032	A&S Hldrs	
Packman, L H W	Pte	6285463	Buffs	
Page, C V	Cpl	7615870	REME	
Palmer, T	Pte	3187342	Gordons	
Parris, T A	Sgn	6345605	RWK	KIA, Bagnara
Payne, P	L/Bdr	987448	RA	
Payne, S	L/Cpl	4922374	RAC	
Phillips, D	Pte	5498990	Hamps	
Poat, H W	Major	123359	KOSB	
Pocock, E	Pte	55437461	KORR	KIA, Termoli
Pond, J	Tpr	7952395	RAC	WIA, Termoli
Powell, T	Sgn	3718414	R. Sigs	
Radley, H	Cpl	5728600	Dorset	
Ralphs, E	L/Cpl	3656776	S. Lancs	
Ransom, T	Gnr	1438601	RA	
Reed, A	Pte	3959174	ACC	

Name	Rank	Army No.	Parent Unit	Notes
Reeves, D	L/Cpl	6016899	Essex	
Rennie, T P	Bdr	1477667	RA	WIA, Termoli
Reynolds, H	Cpl			RTU 8 Aug
Rhodes, F	L/Cpl	2626982	G. Gds	
Richards, C T	Sgn	7955348	RAC	KIA, Bagnara
Ridler, D	L/Cpl	2982024	A&S Hldrs	
Ridler, F	Sgt	2992162	A&S Hldrs	
Riley, C G G	Lt			
Rogerson, A	Pte	2932601	Camerons	
Rose, B	Pte	5182879	DCLI	
Rose, G	WOII (SSM)	2617725	G. Gds	
Sanders, S	L/Cpl	6468171	RF	
Sargent, T	Cpl	7590815	RAOC	
Scherzinger, R J	L/Cpl	1080354	RA	KIA, Termoli
Schofield, A J	L/Sgt	4126106	Life Gds	
Schofield, G	Pte	3533232	Manchester	
Seekings, A R	S/Sgt	5933155	Cambs	
Seekings, R	Pte	5932934	Cambs	
Shaw, C	Sgt	405121	Staffs Yeo	WIA, Bagnara
Shaw, G	Pte	7344428	RAMC	KIA, Augusta
Shirley, L	Pte	5727912	Dorset	
Silifants, S A	L/Cpl	1462315	RA	KIA, Termoli
Sillito, J	Sgt	324811	Staffs Yeo	
Singer	Pte			WIA, Termoli
Skinner, A G	Pte	1883722	RE	WIA, Murro-De-Porco; KIA, Termoli
Smith, A	Pte	7608935	RAOC	

Name	Rank	Army No.	Parent Unit	Notes
Smith, E T	L/Bdr	5949701	RA	
Smith, J	L/Cpl	3323661	HLI	
Smith, R	Pte	3859016	Loyals	
Smith, S	Gnr	1427587	RA	
Squires	Pte			WIA, Bagnara
Stalker, W J	Pte	2931430	L'pl Scots	
Stewart, J	Tpr	7888628	RAC	
Stewart-Johnston, T	Pte	1609969	RA	KIA, Termoli
Storey, J	Sgt	3597146	S. Gds	
Sturmey, K	L/Cpl			WIA, Termoli
Swann, J	L/Cpl			PW, Termoli
Swanson, S	Pte	6968780	RAMC	
Sylvester, F	L/Cpl	5568213	Wilts	
Taggart, B	Cpl	10632215	ACC	
Taylor, A J J	L/Cpl	6014032	Essex	
Telford, J	L/Cpl			
Terry, J	Sgt	880535	RA	WIA, Augusta
Thomas, J	Gnr	1442689	RA	
Thompson, J	L/Cpl			
Thomson, A G	Cpl	5341467	R. Berks	
Thorn, B	L/Cpl	7927715	RAC	
Thurston, A	L/Cpl			WIA, Bagnara
Tideswell, H N	Pte	4976694	Notts & Derby	
Tobin, C F	Gdsm	2719627	Ir. Gds	KIA, Bagnara
Tomlinson, S	Tpr	4690849	RTR	
Tonkin, J E	Capt	200156		PW, Termoli (later escaped)

Name	Rank	Army No.	Parent Unit	Notes
Torrence, C	Fus	6341261	RF	
Trask, D	Pte	7604973	RAOC	
Tunstall	Pte			WIA, Bagnara
Valentine, A	Pte	5945667	Green Howards	
Valentine, R	Pte	2880100	Gordons	
Vango	Pte			WIA, Termoli
Vidler, R	L/Cpl			PW, Termoli
Waddell, J	Pte	2989148	A&S Hldrs	
Weatherhead, S	Pte	2872536	Gordons	
Westover, A	Pte	6410904	Queen's	
White, F H	Sgt	3535141	Loyals	
White, T	Gnr	5381502	RA	
Wilding, J	L/Cpl			WIA, Augusta
Wilmott, R	Pte	213473	ACC	
Wilson, A M	Lt (A/Capt)	203919	Gordons	KIA, Termoli
Wilson, C	Tpr	557904	Notts Yeo	WIA, Bagnara
Wilson, E	L/Cpl	4130949	Cheshire	WIA, Augusta
Wilson, H	Sgt	2614107	G. Gds	
Winn	Pte			PW, Termoli
Wiseman, J M	Capt	256809	DCLI	
Wood, R	L/Cpl			PW, Termoli
Woodhead, J	Gnr	1462622	RA	
Wooten, J	Pte	6019818	Essex	
Wortley, R	Cpl	4863732	W. Yorks	WIA, Bagnara
Younger, J	L/Bdr	1495210	RA	
Youngman, A	L/Cpl	5774993	Norfolk	

Key to Abbreviations

Ranks

Cfn – Craftsman; Dvr – Driver; Fus – Fusilier; Gdsm – Guardsman; Gnr – Gunner; Pte – Private; Rfn – Rifleman; Sgn – Signalman; Spr – Sapper; Tpr - Trooper

L/Bdr – Lance Bombardier; L/Cpl – Lance Corporal; Bdr – Bombardier; Cpl - Corporal

L/Sgt – Lance Sergeant; Sgt – Sergeant; S/Sgt – Staff Sergeant; SQMS – Squadron Quarter Master Sergeant

WO II (CSM) – Warrant Officer, Class II (Company Sergeant Major); WO II (SSM) – Warrant Officer Class II (Squadron Sergeant Major)

Lt – Lieutenant; A/Capt – Acting Captain; Capt – Captain

Regiments/Corps

ACC – Army Catering Corps; APTC – Army Physical Training Corps; A & S Hldrs – Argyll & Sutherland Highlanders; BW – Black Watch; Camerons – Queen's Own Cameron Highlanders; CLY – County of London Yeomanry; DCLI – Duke of Cornwall's Light Infantry; E. Yorks – East Yorkshire Regt; Coldm Gds – Coldstream Guards; DLI – Durham Light Infantry; E. Surrey – East Surrey Regiment; G. Gds – Grenadier Guards; Gordons – Gordon Highlanders; HLI – Highland Light Infantry; Ir. Gds – Irish Guards; KORR – King's Own Royal Regt; KOSB – King's Own Scottish Borderers; L & B Yeo – Lothians and Border Yeomanry; Loyals – Loyal Regt (North Lancashire); Notts & Derby – Sherwood Foresters (Nottinghamshire & Derbyshire Regt); RA – Royal Artillery; RHA – Royal Horse Artillery; RF – Royal Fusiliers; RNF – Royal Northumberland Fusiliers; S. Gds – Scots Guards; RAC – Royal Armoured Corps; RAChD – Royal Army Chaplains Dept; RAMC – Royal Army Medical Corps; RAOC- Royal Army Ordnance Corps; RASC – Royal Army Service Corps; RAVC – Royal Army Veterinary Corps; RB – Rifle Brigade; RE – Royal Engineers; Recce – Reconnaissance Corps; REME – Royal Electrical

& Mechanical Engineers;. R. Sigs – Royal Signals; RTR – Royal Tank Regt; RWK – Royal West Kent Regt; Seaforth – Seaforth Highlanders; UDF – Union Defence Force (S. Africa); W. Gds – Welsh Guards; W. Yorks – West Yorkshire Regt

Hsrs – Hussars; Yeo – Yeomanry

In other cases the regiment's title includes the word, or county abbreviation, shown to which should be added 'Regiment', eg, Devon denotes The Devonshire Regt, R. Sussex The Royal Sussex Regt and Essex The Essex Regt.

Other

Adj – Adjutant; KIA – Killed in action; PW – Prisoner of war; RFHQ – Raiding Forces Headquarters; RTU – Returned to unit; SOS – Struck off strength; WIA – Wounded in action

Appendix IV

Recommendation for the Victoria Cross
Lieutenant-Colonel R.B. Mayne

S. A. S.	Brigade	—	Division	Br Airborne	Corps		Received		Passed

Schedule No. .... Unit 1 Special Air Service Regt
(To be left blank)

Rank and Army or Personal No. W/Major (T/Lt Col) 87306

Name .... MAYNE   Robert Blair   DSO and 2 Bars
(Christian names must be stated)

Action for which commended (Date and place of action must be stated)	Recommended by	Honour or Reward	(To be left blank)

On Monday April 9th 1945, Lt Col R.B. Mayne was ordered
by the GOC 4th Canadian Armoured Division to lead his
Regt (then consisting of two Armd Jeep Sqns) through the
British lines and infiltrate through the German lines.
His general axis of adv was NE towards the city of
Oldenburg, with the special task of clearing a path for
the Canadian armd cars and tanks, and also causing alarm
and disorganisation behind the enemy lines. As subsequent events proved, the task of Lt Col Mayne's force was
entirely and completely successful. This success however
was solely due to the brilliant mil leadership and cool
calculating courage of Lt Col Mayne who, by a single act
of supreme bravery drove the enemy from a strongly held
key village, thereby breaking the crust of the enemy
defences in the whole of this sector. The following is a
detailed account of the Lt Col's individual action, which
called for both unsurpassed Heroism and cool clear -
sighted mil knowledge:-   Lt Col Mayne on receiving a
wireless message from the leading sqn reporting that it
was heavily engaged by enemy fire and that the sqn Comd
had been killed, immediately drove forward to the scene
of the action. From the time of his arrival until the
end of the action Lt Col Mayne was in full view of the

enemy and exposed to fire from small arms, machine-guns, ...er's rifles and panzerfausts.
On arrival he sum—— the situation in a matter of sec. and entered the nearest house
alone (house C) and ...sured that the enemy here had either withdrawn or been killed. He then
seized a Bren gun and magazines and single-handed fired burst after burst into the second
house (house D) killing and wounding all the enemy here and also opening fire on the wood
(F). He then ordered a jeep to come forward and take over his fire position, he himself
returning to the forward section where he disposed the men to the best advantage and
and ordered another jeep to come forward. He got in the jeep and with another Offr as
rear-gunner drove forward past the posn where the Sqn Comd had been killed a few minutes
previously and continued to a point a hundred yards ahead, where a further section of jeeps
were halted by intense and accurate enemy fire. This section had suffered casualties in killed
and wounded owing to the heavy enemy fire and the survivors were unable at the time to
influence the action in any way until the arrival of Lt Col Mayne. The Lt Col continued
along the road all the time engaging the enemy with fire from his own jeep. Having swept the
whole area very thoroughly with close-range fire, he turned his jeep round and drove back
again down the road, still in full view of the enemy. By this time the enemy had suffered
heavy casualties and were starting to withdraw. Nevertheless they maintained an accurate
fire on the road and it appeared almost impossible to extricate the wounded who were in the
ditch near the forward jeeps. Any attempt at rescuing these men under these conditions
appeared virtually suicidal owing to the highly concentrated and accurate fire of the Germans.
Though he fully realised the risk he was taking Lt Col Mayne turned his jeep round once again
and returned to try and rescue these wounded. Then by superlative determination and by dis-
playing gallantry of the very highest degree and in the face of intense enemy machine-gun fire
he lifted the wounded one by one into the jeep, turned round and drove back to the main body.
The entire enemy posn had been wiped out, the majority of the enemy having been killed or
wounded, leaving a very small remnant who were now in full retreat. The Sqn having suffered
no further casualties, were able to continue their adv and drive deeper behind the enemy lines
to complete their task of sabotage and destruction of the enemy. Finally they reached a
point 20 miles ahead of the adv guard of the advancing Canadian Div thus threatening the
rear of the Germans, who finally withdrew. From the time of the arrival of Lt Col Mayne,
his cool and determined action and his complete command of the situation together with his
unsurpassed gallantry, inspired all ranks. Not only did he save the lives of the wounded but
also completely defeated and destroyed the enemy.

1199

208/Officers Gen/1 C
Hq 3 Cdn Inf Div COF
20 Jun 45

Comd 2 Cdn Corps

VICTORIA CROSS
Lt-Col R.B. MAYNE, DSO

1.   My orders to Lt-Col MAYNE on 9 Apr 45 were
to pass through my leading tps when they had established
a crossing over the EMS at MEPPEN, then to penetrate
quickly and deeply into the enemy rear areas in the
direction of OLDENBERG. You will remember that the
fighting was very fluid at that time and my division
was making daily adv of 25 to 50 miles. I did not tie
MAYNE down to routes, and he accepted the task with
enthusiasm and alacrity.

2.   The following day we captured MEPPEN established a bridge and re-commenced the advance. In the
meantime MAYNE slipped his force through and I heard no
more from him for over 48 hours, when my leading elements caught up with him in the area of ESTEWEGEN -
LORUP a straight line distance of 25 to 30 miles from
MEPPEN.

3.   I learned then that his force had had some
severe fighting were out of amn and food and at one time
had over 400 prisoners of assorted shapes and sizes.
They had disarmed the lot, had held about 100 of the
toughest type, mostly, paratps, and had chased the others
back in the general direction of our adv. This had been
slowed somewhat by determined enemy resistance in SOGEL
and along the line of the KUSTEN KANAL.

4.   It is my opinion that Lt-Col MAYNE's spirited
leadership and dash were a most important contribution to
the success of the operations. It was no easy task which
I had asked him to perform.

5.   I cannot produce any Canadian eye witnesses to
his personal acts of bravery as his force was operating
entirely on its own. When visiting his unit, however, I
observed the very marked respect and regard in which he
was held by his officers and men.

6.   In my opinion this officer is worthy of the
highest award for gallantry and leadership.

[signature]

(C Vokes) Maj-Gen
GOC 3 Cdn Inf Div COF

/fp

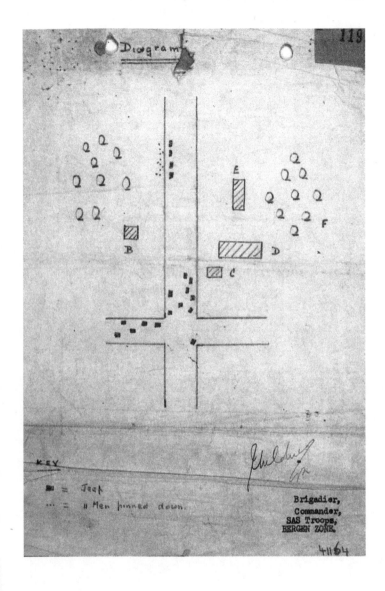

Index

Persons

Index

General